WHY DIDN'T I THINK OF THAT?

WHY DIDN'T I THINK OF THAT?

Bizarre Origins of Ingenious Inventions We Couldn't Live Without

Allyn Freeman
Bob Golden

John Wiley & Sons, Inc.

New York • Chichester • Weinheim • Brisbane • Singapore • Toronto

Copyright © 1997 by Allyn Freeman & Bob Golden.
Published by John Wiley & Sons, Inc.

This publication is designed to provide accurate and authoritative
information in regard to the subject matter covered. It is sold
with the understanding that the publisher is not engaged in
rendering legal, accounting, or other professional services. If
legal advice or other expert assistance is required, the services
of a competent professional person should be sought.

Library of Congress Cataloging-in-Publication Data:
Freeman, Allyn.
     Why didn't I think of that? : bizarre origins of ingenious
inventions we couldn't live without / by Allyn Freeman & Bob Golden.
     p. cm.
     Includes bibliographical references and index.
     ISBN 0-471-16511-5
     1. Inventions—History. I. Golden, Bob. II. Title.
T15.F615   1997
   608—DC21   97-7700
Printed in the United States of America
10 9 8 7 6 5 4 3 2 1

CONTENTS

INTRODUCTION   ix

1   **GROUNDS FOR SUCCESS**   1
     MELITTA, INC.

2   **WORLD ON A STRING**   5
     DUNCAN YO-YO

3   **PARTY TIME!**   10
     TUPPERWARE

4   **NATURE'S PURIFIER**   16
     EX-LAX

5   **MALE-BONDING**   20
     ELMER'S ALL-PURPOSE GLUE

6   **$AFE $EX**   25
     TROJAN CONDOMS

7   **BIG RED**   31
     HEINZ KETCHUP

8   **MAKE NO MISTAKE**   36
     LIQUID PAPER

9   **TABBY TOILET**   41
     KITTY LITTER

10   **A PEACEFUL PERIOD**   46
     TAMPAX

11   **THE WRIGHT STUFF**   51
     SILLY PUTTY

12   **MEDICAL COVERAGE**   56
BAND-AID

13   **IN THE CARDS**   60
HALLMARK, INC.

14   **INDOOR SKI SENSATION**   65
NORDICTRACK

15   **THOU SHALT NOT STEAL**   70
THE CLUB

16   **THE CUTTING EDGE**   74
CUISINART, INC.

17   **WONDER JELLY**   78
VASELINE

18   **SILENCE IS GOLDEN**   83
MIDAS

19   **MINI MASTER BUILDERS**   87
LEGO

20   **LET THE GAMES BEGIN**   91
TRIVIAL PURSUIT

21   **IN-JEAN-IOUS**   95
LEVI STRAUSS & COMPANY

22   **GET A GRIP**   99
VELCRO

23   **WHEELS OF FORTUNE**   104
ROLLERBLADES, INC.

24   **CLEAN SWEEP**   109
THE DIRT DEVIL

25   **BILLION DOLLAR DOLLY**   113
BARBIE

26   **LOVIN' SPOONFUL**   117
JELL-O

27 PEN PAL   122
BIC

28 THE COLOR OF MONEY   126
CLAIROL

29 SOME LIKE IT HOT   131
TABASCO SAUCE

30 SPRING FEVER   136
SLINKY

31 RUNNING HOT AND COLD   141
THERMOS

32 LITTLE VITTLES   146
GERBER

33 STOCKING STUFFER   151
L'EGGS

34 IN THE CHIPS   156
FRITO-LAY

35 BOTTOMS UP   162
PAMPERS

36 EASY LISTENING   167
BELTONE

37 PADS OF GLORY   172
S.O.S

38 THE YELLOW PAGES   176
POST-IT NOTES

39 LITTLE DIPPER   180
DIXIE CUPS

40 HOUSE OF WAX   185
CRAYOLA

41 THE CANDY MAN   190
TOOTSIE ROLL

42   **A STITCH IN TIME**   194
SINGER SEWING MACHINE

43   **HOME COOKING**   199
BOSTON MARKET

44   **CURRENT SUCCESS**   203
JACUZZI

45   **THE CHAIRMEN**   207
LA-Z-BOY

46   **MORNING STAR**   211
KELLOGG'S CORN FLAKES

47   **SLICE OF LIFE**   216
SWISS ARMY KNIFE

48   **HILL OF BEANS**   220
STARBUCKS

49   **THE BIG CHILL**   225
BEN & JERRY'S ICE CREAM

50   **POCKET BOOK**   231
FILOFAX

ACKNOWLEDGMENTS   235

BIBLIOGRAPHY   237

INDEX   239

INTRODUCTION

Remember that day when you spotted the newspaper article of a new product in the marketplace and your surprised reaction was, "Hey, I thought of that!" And maybe you did. The difference is that other people with more motivation, more experience, and perhaps more capital converted that original idea into reality. They'll go on to riches and fame and you'll forever wonder what might have happened had you been more entrepreneurial.

Where do new products and inventions come from? Why do they succeed? How do people, many just plain folks with average business skills, capitalize on an idea that makes them millionaires? These questions intrigued us and we decided to write a book to learn the answers.

SEARCHING FOR THE PERFECT PRODUCTS

At the outset, we compiled a list of 200 possible products, with plans to reduce the list to a workable 50. We eliminated those suited for scientific journals like the X-ray, cellular phone, and plastic food wrap, or others whose stories have been overexposed in the media like Microsoft, Apple Computer, and McDonald's. Eventually, we agreed on the following criteria:

1. An individual made a great deal of money from the product (preferably, but not exclusively, the creator or inventor).

2. The product's name would be instantly recognizable.

3. The stories would contain historical and quirky facts.

INTRODUCTION

GATHERING RESEARCH MATERIAL

o find the most intriguing stories of the most ingenious creations, we asked friends and family for suggestions. Many sent back a diverse list of recommendations. All included the legendary Post-Its from the 3M Company. (Turn to page 176 for more details about this "divinely inspired" idea.) We eliminated stories that didn't meet our three criteria or were put-you-to-sleep boring. At this point, our research took the following form:

- We contacted the public relations departments at the corporations. Who better to supply financial, advertising, and marketing material? Most willingly sent us historical information, especially the originas of the products.

- We visited the New York Public Library's Business Branch to read previously published works about inventors and inventions, and to find data from reference and business encyclopedias. We also plumbed the Internet, finding many websites for companies and products.

- With the research material reaching critical mass, the last step was to begin writing the engrossing tales of the people who created, invented, or profited from products we couldn't live without.

THEIR PATH TO RICHES

e formulated three possible methods for how people made money and, surprisingly, two did not require individual creativity or inventive talent.

INTRODUCTION

THE FIRST ONES IN—
INVENTORS AND CREATORS

Some stories chronicle people who succeeded due to a brilliant stroke of genius that came by accident or by design. Two examples are Liquid Paper, an item anyone could have discovered, and Velcro, which only a scientist could have created.

Think of the billions of nail polish bottles opened, used, and discarded. Only Bette Nesmith refilled an empty bottle with diluted white paint to erase typewriter errors. When she died, her estate totaled more than $50 million.

Imagine over the years the millions of clinging cockleburs people plucked from wool clothing. Only an engineer examined the burr under a microscope and wondered whether a synthetic cloth could bind together without fasteners. George de Mestral, inventor of Velcro, lived in a Swiss castle.

THE SECOND ONES IN—
"I SPY WITH MY ENTREPRENEURIAL EYE"

A second method was to spot the light bulb that went off over someone else's head. Occasionally, this occurred as a person was searching for a new product or business. Every once in a while, it occurred by happenstance.

A Frenchman, tired of expensive ballpoint pens that smeared, decided to make a more reliable and cheaper pen. Marcel Bich sailed racing yachts in the America's Cup races and his Bic company generates more than $1 billion annually.

INTRODUCTION

A man drove down a street and stopped to watch a boy perform odd tricks with a ball-and-string device. Later, he purchased the toy's patent and the yo-yo made Donald Duncan rich and famous.

THIRD ONES IN—
MARKETERS AND CAPITALISTS

third avenue was to purchase the stock of a fledgling company and then, through marketing and financial savvy, make it profitable. The inventors of Rollerblade had moderate success selling inline skates. But Robert Naegele, who purchased control of the company for $250,000, sold his stock for $150 million.

Tampax traded hands three times before a seasoned New York-based advertising expert turned it into the giant company called Tambrands.

WHAT WE FOUND:
A PREVIEW IN QUIZ FORM

ach day, fascinating facts passed our desks. Why the muffler franchise is named Midas. The oriental origins of the word ketchup. Why the coffee filters are called Melitta and many more quirky tidbits.

The following test previews what you'll read about in this book.

A.   Mahatma Gandhi said of a product:

    1.   "I love to spice up my vegetarian curry with Heinz Ketchup."

2. "For repairing sandals, nothing works better than Elmer's Glue."

3. "The sewing machine was one of the few useful things ever invented."

B. The Swiss Army Knife was invented because:

1. The Swiss Army used a knife manufactured in Germany.

2. The existing knife did not contain a nasal hair clipper.

3. Americans needed an unusual bar mitzvah gift.

C. The success of Silly Putty was directly a result of:

1. An Easter Egg hunt on the White House lawn in the Truman years.

2. An article that appeared in The New Yorker's "Talk of the Town" section.

3. Lucky Pup plastering it over Foudini's face on a 1949 kids' television show.

FINAL WORDS

Learning about these products transported us on a historic trip through place and time. We began in 1818 at the Avery Plantation in Louisiana, future home of Tabasco Sauce, and continued to 1985 with the introduction of Boston Chicken restaurants. We traveled to the Arctic with Thermos and to the Moon with Silly Putty. In the past two centuries, we witnessed how Americans changed their habits after the introduction of Trojan Condoms, Hallmark Cards, and Dixie Cups.

Do we have a few favorites? Two facts brought instant laughs: The original name of Ex-Lax was BoBo and a 1789 painting in the Louvre is called, "Nobleman with his Yo-Yo."

INTRODUCTION

Inspiration comes in many shapes. When you're part of a writing team hoping to garner riches beyond avarice, inspiration often came at lunch. Once, while dining at an Upper Westside restaurant on Broadway, inspiration was delivered in a chicken Shawarma sandwich (served on pita bread with Mid-Eastern spices). This tasty creation prompted the notion that we could make a fortune franchising a national chain of Shawarma Shacks.

If the fantasy of becoming instant Shawarma millionaires doesn't pan out, we have high hopes this book will turn into a "best-seller."

Allyn Freeman and Bob Golden
New York City
June 1997

WHY DIDN'T I THINK OF THAT?

GROUNDS FOR SUCCESS

MELITTA, INC.

FOR COFFEE MAKING, MAMA KNEW BEST

It's 1908, you're Frau Bentz, a German hausfrau, 35-years-old with a loving husband and two dutiful sons. You invite some Dresden ladies over to your house on Marschallstrasse for coffee and cake and to give thanks that Kaiser Bill's sitting on the Imperial throne. The afternoon *Kaffeeklatsch* is a big success and the women praise your *apfel torte* to the sky. The one sour note was rung by Frau Von Molte who mutters that the coffee tastes a tad bitter. Then there was pretty Fraulein Glassburg who looks slightly ridiculous when she smiles and specks of black coffee grounds ruin the line of her shiny white teeth.

Frau Bentz decided then and there to find a solution to these pesky problems of coffeemaking: Instead of putting the coffee grounds *inside* an enclosed receptacle, she nestled them in a filter apparatus *outside*. The result was the perfect cup of coffee—and the start of a billion-dollar brand name which would, in its familiar red and green package, become known and used throughout the world: **Melitta.**

Melitta earns over $1.6 billion per year, and is still controlled by Frau Bentz's grandsons, operating out of Minden, Germany, and Clearwater, Florida.

GROUNDS FOR SUCCESS

COFFEE: AN AROMATIC HISTORY

Coffee originated in Ethiopia around 575 BC, and soon travelled to the Arab world—hence the genus and species name: *coffee arabica*. Coffee, a name derived from the Arab *Qahwah,* and the Turkish *kahveh,* became in Europe café, coffee, and Kaffee.

By the seventeenth century English coffee houses replaced chocolate houses as a place for men to congregate, do business, and imbibe this popular (and then-believed medicinal) brew. So popular was the drink and the social life that grew up around it that, in 1674, a booklet appeared in London called *A Woman's Petition against Coffee,* which lamented that men spent all their spare time in coffee houses, where drinking more than two cups rendered them impotent.

Seventy-five percent of all home-brewed coffee in the United States is made using the **drip filter** method.

Until 1800, the infusion method of coffeemaking prevailed in Europe, when the Archbishop of Paris invented a drip pot which was called a *percolateur.* Forty years later, a Scottish marine engineer named Robert Napier perfected a vacuum and glass apparatus that forced water over the grinds.

At the turn of the last century, brewed coffee was made either by boiling grounds inside a metal or porcelain sleeve, or by pouring hot water over grounds encased in a cloth bag. To Germans, this seemed a more refined way than a French technique of brewing coffee in old socks. But no matter which method was used, the resultant coffee was cloudy and acid-tasting; or the process took so long the coffee turned cold before it could be consumed. The world was ready for a simple and economical way to make delicious coffee, every time.

GROUNDS FOR SUCCESS

MAMA AND PAPA GO TO THE FAIR

With her filter idea in mind, Frau Bentz went to her son's room, searching for some type of absorbent paper. After rejecting some as too thin or too thick, she settled on blotting paper. Carefully, she measured out some coffee grounds, set them over the paper, poured in boiling water and watched it drip slowly through a small brass pot she drilled with small holes on the bottom. She watched with delight as the porcelain pot filled with aromatic coffee free of loose grounds. And the first taste of her invention? *Wunderbar!* Paper and pot proved to be the ideal filter and receptacle.

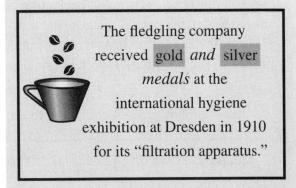

The fledgling company received gold *and* silver *medals* at the international hygiene exhibition at Dresden in 1910 for its "filtration apparatus."

Her next step was to patent the invention. In 1908, at Berlin's Royal Patent Office, she staked her claim on a brass "coffee filter with filtration paper." She and her husband Hugo hired a tinsmith to produce high-walled brass tops. A local art supply house provided the filter paper. Following some local success, the energetic Frau Bentz had caught the entrepreneurial bug. She wanted to sell the coffee filtration system to all of Germany. The Bentzes took their life savings and rented a small booth at the 1909 Trade Fair in Leipzig.

With its combination of elegance and practicality, the Melitta coffeemaking method caught on. The brass pot had an easy-to-hold handle, and fit smartly atop coffeepots. But most important, the coffee tasted delicious. The Bentzes had hoped to break even and generate a little publicity. Instead, they sold a remarkable 1,200 Melitta filtration systems in a week!

GROUNDS FOR SUCCESS

EUROPE: COMING 'ROUND THE BENTZ

By 1925, with German sales soaring, Melitta found itself in danger from competition. To distinquish itself from imitation, Frau Bentz decided to design a memorable packaging color scheme, making it easier for consumers to find in stores. She chose the now-famous red and green that, when combined with rich coffee brown, represented the perfect color for quality coffee products. The trademark logo was established in 1932.

As the company grew, it continued to improve its filtration system, resulting in the familiar conical filter with inner-wall grooves, patented in 1937. The brass top was replaced by white porcelain with a protective aluminum covering. The development of heat-resistant plastics led to the indestructible lightweight filter; and later still, the single person's morning pal, the handy 1x, one-cup filter was added to the line.

> Melitta opened a chain of Coffee World espresso bars in U.S. shopping malls. The goal is to have **100 to 200** in operation before the year 2000.

THE SURPRISE ENDING

Frau Bentz changed forever the way the world would make and enjoy coffee. Her simple creation earned millions for the Bentz family—and still does, as grandsons Jörg, Thomas, and Stephan continue to run the worldwide family business. Her coffee filtration system also made a profound personal statement, rare for a woman in 1908. She immortalized her achievement by naming the company after herself: Frau Melitta Bentz.

WORLD ON A STRING
DUNCAN YO-YO

"SLEEPING" ON THE JOB

At some point in history, a little round toy on a string called a *bandalore* by Europeans made its way to China, and eventually, via the Asian Sea trade routes, into the Philippines. The *bandalore* was nothing more than a circular disk that rolled down the end of a hand-held string and then returned. The Filipinos improved on the model by looping the string around the axle, which allowed the toy to "rest" at the end of its string before the disk returned upward.

Fast-forward to Santa Monica, California, and the late 1920s. Pedro Flores, a Filipino busboy at a local hotel, was a yo-yo expert who could make the toy do amazing things and often entertained countryfolk with his tricks. He registered the toy with the U.S. Patent office under the name Flores Yo-Yo and began producing hand-crafted wooden models. One day, Donald F. Duncan, Sr. stopped on a street corner to watch with fascination as a yo-yo aficionado made the toy "sleep"— rest at the end of its string. By 1932, he had purchased the rights and the trademark from Flores and started to manufacture an all-American standard: the **Duncan Yo-Yo.**

"Yo-yo" means *"come back, come back"* in the native Philippine language of Tagalog.

WORLD ON A STRING

YO-YO YESTERDAYS

Asian historians would have the world believe that the yo-yo dates back to Stone Age tribes in the Philippines. Tribesmen attached "hunting rocks" to long strings made from plant fibers and animal hide. These hunter-hurlers would fling the projectiles at prey, and the rock, presumably hand-picked for the purpose, would not be lost forever on the jungle floor.

In fact, the first historical reference to a yo-yo dates to 450 BC in Greece. A bowl from that time and place shows a boy playing with a disk dangling on the end of a string. Today, documentation further indicates that the toy was popular in the royal courts of France and England in the sixteenth and seventeenth century, where it went by many exotic names such as *quiz, l'emigrette, coblentz,* and *incroyable.*

Even Napoleon's armies passed the time between eating veal Marengo and conquering Europe by playing with the toy. In the late eighteenth century, a yo-yo craze hit Paris. Many French nobles had theirs crafted of intricately carved ivory or delicate glass, with polished brass axles. Across the Channel, Lord Wellington, the Iron Duke of England, is reputed to have been a yo-yo aficionado.

> The yo-yo is the second oldest toy; only dolls are older. The largest collection of yo-yos belongs to a Florida dermatologist who has over 4,000 different ones.

Traditionally, though, the world's yo-yo experts have been men and boys in the Philippines, for whom the toy became a national pastime. They carved their disks out of caribou horn or lignum, known as the wood of life. And when, after the Spanish-American War, many Philippine natives emigrated to California, they brought with them their culture, which included the yo-yo.

WORLD ON A STRING

DUNCAN HIRES

Donald Duncan continued to make the Flores yo-yo out of indigenous hardwoods—maple, ash, and beechwood. He kept the basic shape and size, leaving it small enough to fit comfortably in the palm of a hand.

Duncan realized that a magazine illustration depicting a boy playing with the toy would elicit reader interest but few sales. He knew that the yo-yo had to be seen in action to be appreciated. Thus he decided to replicate the moment in which his enthusiasm had been triggered: America would see Filipino yo-yo aces in action. Duncan visited the Filipino neighborhoods in southern California and hired dozens of local champs to promote his yo-yo.

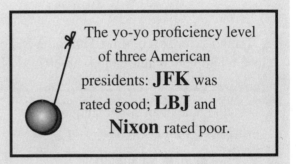

The yo-yo proficiency level of three American presidents: **JFK** was rated good; **LBJ** and **Nixon** rated poor.

During the 1930s, groups of these Filipino yo-yo experts would appear outside local candy stores or movie houses, where they would perform a kind of street theater for the assembled crowds. City kids mesmerized by these gravity-defying tricks could purchase a Duncan Yo-Yo at the local neighborhood candy store or five-and-ten only a short walk away.

Sales rose in great part as a result of these demonstrations, but Duncan wanted a faster way to promote his yo-yo and found the perfect, if unlikely, partner in William Randolph Hearst. The media mogul agreed to advertise Duncan's yo-yo contests with the proviso that any kid who wanted to enter had to sell three subscriptions to any Hearst newspaper. One of the first promotions of this kind occurred in Philadelphia in 1931 and resulted in the astonishing sale of 3 million Duncan Yo-Yos.

WORLD ON A STRING

RISE AND FALL AND RISE

he yo-yo even succeeded during the Great Depression because it was inexpensive, fun, and long-lasting. If a string broke, it could be replaced for less than a penny. The hardwood construction also survived hours of "walking the dog" on asphalt and cement. It was a great value when the long years of constant use were calculated against the low purchase price.

The yo-yo craze continued until the end of World War II, when the toy started to lose its appeal as television advertised new toys to a wider audience. Duncan didn't catch on until 1962, when he too used the new medium. Sales again skyrocketed, reaching an all-time peak of 33 million units in 1963. But as the cost of network television commercials increased in the 1970s and 1980s, the inexpensively made Duncan Yo-Yo was faced with prohibitive advertising costs and diminishing profit margins. Without seeing the toy in action, sales plummeted to a paltry 500,000 per year.

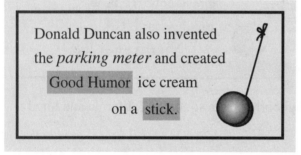

Donald Duncan also invented the *parking meter* and created Good Humor ice cream on a stick.

Indirectly, it was media tycoon Ted Turner who helped save the toy. Cable television advertising, particularly on shows targeted to children, proved more affordable for Duncan. Soon, 30-second commercials saturated cable stations. Duncan Yo-Yo sales rebounded again.

WORLD ON A STRING

YO-YO VERSUS YO-YO

Duncan Toys was always cognizant it had an attenuated claim to the yo-yo name, and with over 85 percent of market sales, it virtually owned the trademark. But in 1965, the Federal Court of Appeals in Chicago ruled against Duncan Toys and for the Royal Tops Company, which sought to use the name. Yo-yo was deemed a generic term for the toy, meaning anyone could use it.

PLASTIC FUTURE FOR THE FLYWHEEL

In 1957, the Flambeau Plastics Company in Baraboo, Wisconsin, made the first plastic Duncan Yo-Yos in the same form and size as the famous original wooden model, the Duncan 77. Flambeau purchased Duncan Toys in 1968, and today makes approximately 70,000 yo-yos per day.

Scientists refer to the yo-yo as "kinetic energy in a rotating mass—a toy flywheel." But for American kids since 1930, the Duncan Yo-Yo has been a source of endless hours of fun and enjoyment.

PARTY TIME!
TUPPERWARE

BEHIND EVERY MAN IS A WOMAN...
WITH A BETTER IDEA

n 1939, Earl Tupper was a self-taught inventor who convinced Du Pont to sell him some left-over synthetic material. Taking a mass of smelly polyethylene waste product, Tupper developed a new refining process that purified the slag into a clear, flexible, unbreakable, nontoxic, lightweight, and easy-to-clean plastic. In 1947, he started making and marketing food storage containers out of the stuff, selling directly to stores. Then one day, in 1949, he answered a telephone call from his southern Florida distributor, a woman named Brownie Wise, who complained that his slow shipments were hindering her expansion. He looked at her sales figures, astonished to see they totalled a hefty $1,500 weekly and asked, "What's the secret of your success?" Her one-sentence reply—"I sell the products on a party plan"—would radically change the way a nation stored food. Her idea would make **Tupperware** a household name and Earl Tupper a multimillionaire.

> Earl Tupper's first creations in clear and pastel colors were placed in permanent collection in the **Museum of Modern Art** and the **Smithsonian.**

PARTY TIME!

PLASTICITY

Plastics—derived from the Greek word *plastikos,* for "molding"—initially were not an easy sell to Americans, who were accustomed to using natural products made from wood or metal. Homemakers at first were reluctant to buy items made of this synthetic material with its shiny veneer and cold touch. Even Logan Gourlay's quote in *Webster's New Abridged Dictionary* (1976) reinforced the perception of the synthetic's mass-produced, inferior quality: "This is the plastic age, the era of the sham and the bogus."

Plastic dates back to the nineteenth century, with the discovery of celluloid, a durable material made from cellulose nitrate and camphor. The one glaring problem with celluloid was that it was flammable. Its first practical use was as handles for flatware; heat-resistant Bakelite marked the next improvement. But the 1930s ushered in the renaissance of plastic inventions, introducing to the world cellophane, nylon, Plexiglas, and polystyrene.

Snobbish yachters derisively refer to fiberglass boats as "the Tupperware fleet."

ALL DRESSED UP WITH NO PLACE TO GO

During World War II, Tupper continued to experiment with different plastic containers made from his new process, demonstrating a keen eye for practical and aesthetic design. For Tupper, form followed function, and each container became an ingenious and attractive method for food storage. In the early 1950s, *House Beautiful* magazine praised Tupperware products as "fine art for 39 cents." Tupperware kitchen containers made from precision-injection molding offered another consumer benefit: It was unbreakable. Kick it and it would bounce; squeeze it and, magically, it returned to its original shape.

PARTY TIME!

Only one improvement eluded the clever Tupper: making the lid airtight. In his search for a solution, he studied other products and ultimately designed a variation of the method used to seal paint cans. He reversed the design of the paint can lid, making a seal that was virtually airtight. The recommended release of air gave rise to the famous Tupperware "burp."

It seemed to Earl Tupper that the time had come for his attractive and functional line of plastic food storage containers. But he had one more hurdle to clear: teaching the target consumer how to use his product.

A WISE IDEA

Meanwhile, back in Detroit, Brownie Wise, the party plan aficionado, desperately needed extra income. She was a single mother with a big mortgage and an ill son. She began selling Stanley Home Products and West Bend appliances by party plan, a sales format conceived in the 1920s to introduce aluminum cookware. When a friend gave her Tupperware as a gift, it took Wise three days to figure out how to burp the container. But once she did, she added Tupperware to her product line. When she moved to Miami for her son's health, she said, "I found a warehouse for Tupperware before I moved into a house."

Earl Tupper appointed her vice president and general manager of the company when he realized that Wise had found the best method to sell Tupperware to the consumer. It is the rare entrepreneur who finds the perfect "right hand," whose singular sales and marketing vision vaults the company from penury to profit. But Tupper, a shy person who eschewed the limelight,

Some Tupperware sales reps **earn** over **$100,000 per year**.

PARTY TIME!

recognized that this determined woman was the right person for his operation, especially since women giving "home demonstrations" made up the company's salesforce.

Wise was a direct marketing pioneer; she developed a recruiting, selling, and even peer training system that became the model for many companies. In Orlando, Florida, she oversaw the building of a combination headquarters and campus facility. Then, she instituted a recognition, praise, and reward plan to encourage housewives to participate. When she realized that many women wanted to do more than host the parties, she created management and distribution positions.

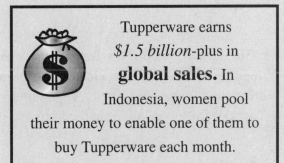

Tupperware earns *$1.5 billion*-plus in **global sales.** In Indonesia, women pool their money to enable one of them to buy Tupperware each month.

Wise assumed the general manager's position in 1951, when Tupperware had 200 independent dealers. Three years later, the sales network had grown to 9,000. Her faith in the Tupperware system was simple: "If we build the people, they'll build the business."

THE "T" PARTIES

The phenomenal success of Tupperware in the 1950s cannot be understood without recognizing the societal changes brought about by the mass migration to the suburbs. Married women found themselves living in new housing tracts outside cities, forced to drive everywhere for shopping and schools. One suburbanite wit wrote, "I dreamed I died and God said, 'Judy, can you carpool in Heaven?'" Missing for many suburban women was a sense of shared community.

PARTY TIME!

Enter the Tupperware Party into these housing developments. Wise and her Florida staff created a perfect pretext under which women could get together while the kids were at school. The afternoon experience—part coffee klatsch, all sell—was carefully scripted to include games, contests, prizes, and surprises. Lasting for as long as two hours, the party format broke down sales resistance. The company brochure touted these events as "thoroughly happy occasions" during which a housewife could combine "a neighborly visit with armchair shopping."

But the main reason for Tupperware's success was that the containers filled an important niche. Modern electric refrigerators generated low temperatures, and dried out uncovered food. Vegetables wilted. Cheese went sour. Airtight Tupperware solved all these food-storage problems.

Earl Tupper also demonstrated creative genius in naming each plastic item separately and distinctly. The first two products were called the Wonderlier Bowl and the Bell Tumbler. Later, the com-

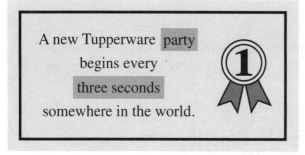

A new Tupperware party begins every three seconds somewhere in the world.

pany introduced the Party Bowl, the Pie Taker, and the Dip 'n Serve. Housewives obliged by using the names and when the next party rolled around, friends could easily order these items by their catchy monikers.

The airtight vacuum created inside the container became the stuff of legend. Letters to the company touted the preservative nature of the lid. Scuba divers found Tupperware containers with cookies almost as fresh as the day they were baked. But the longevity prize goes to the woman who stored shredded coconut in her freezer for 34 years.

PARTY TIME!

EARL SELLS OUT

Although the suburban population of the United States tripled by 1980, sales of Tupperware leveled off because many women were now working part-time or full-time outside the home; and other similar plastic container products were now available in retail outlets. The Tupperware 1950s Ozzie-and-Harriet image was a thing of the past.

In response, Tupperware moved the party plan concept into the workforce and began publishing a direct mail catalog. But its single largest sales generator came through export abroad. The future, yet to be tapped in India and China, remains promising.

In 1958, Earl Tupper sold the company to the Rexall Drug Company for $9 million. In that milestone year Wise also left the company. Tupper retired to Costa Rica and died in 1983, not a bad ending for a high school graduate who created, as stated in the book *American Plastics—A Cultural History*, "a line of products that served to domesticate plastics more than anything else since nylon."

NATURE'S PURIFIER
EX-LAX

KISS AND TELL THE WORLD

Max Kiss emigrated from Hungary to the United States in 1898. He secured an apprentice position with a druggist in New York City and later attended Columbia University's College of Pharmacy, graduating with a degree in 1904. On a return trip to Europe in 1905, Kiss learned that phenolphthalein, a new, tasteless powder manufactured by Bayer, the German aspirin company, was being prescribed as laxative. Having already recognized that the future of medications was in over-the-counter remedies, Kiss set about finding a way to use phenolphthalein in a palatable formulation for just such a remedy. After a year of trying different formulas, combining the laxative powder with different flavor bases, he finally hit upon a chocolate tablet that tasted good, even to children. Now all he needed was a memorable brand name under which to launch the new cathartic. While reading an article in a local Hungarian language newspaper, he spotted the contraction of a slang phrase that meant "parliamentary deadlock." But Kiss also saw a distinctive, easy-to-remember English-language abbreviation for his new product: "excellent laxative"—**Ex-Lax.**

> The first brand name Kiss chose for Ex-Lax was **Bo-Bo.**

NATURE'S PURIFIER

KEEPING REGULAR

The ritual of keeping regular has been a regular ritual since the beginning of time. Over the centuries, humans have turned to natural remedies to restore the process when it was out of whack. Homeopathic and Old World medications relied on plant extracts to relieve constipation, two of the oldest of which were infusions made with senna leaves and lycopodium, the latter a club moss found on evergreen trees. Later, in the eighteenth century, castor oil, the well-known substance made from castor beans, was used as both a purgative and a lubricant. Minerals, too, were found to have properties that alleviated this human discomfort. The most widely known were mineral oil, citrate of magnesia, and milk of magnesia, made from magnesium hydroxide. These plant and mineral purgatives tasted awful.

But phenolphthalein, derived from a crystalline compound, was tasteless. Interestingly, European wine makers mixed the ingredient into their wines to gauge the acidity content. When drinkers reported a mild cathartic effect after drinking wine with the additive, Bayer & Company began to inform physicians of its newly discovered laxative capabilities.

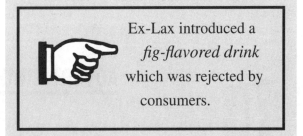

Ex-Lax introduced a *fig-flavored drink* which was rejected by consumers.

TO THE MAX AND BEYOND

Kiss received financial backing from Israel Matz, an interesting Lithuanian immigrant who had become a successful drug wholesaler in Manhattan. Although both men were European immigrants, they had become sufficiently Americanized to understand that tastes in the new country differed from those in the old. And the taste the team of Matz and Kiss was counting on was chocolate.

NATURE'S PURIFIER

The men incorporated in 1906 and opened a small factory in Brooklyn, New York. The first tin package of Ex-Lax was designed with a dark blue background highlighted by an off-white logo outlined in blue. It was an immediate sensation with a tablet form that made it easy to carry to work or school. The chocolate taste also proved to be a favorite with children.

Ex-Lax has been *America's* best selling laxative since 1926. Its most successful promotional gimmick was a free temperature thermometer.

The clever name also made the product easy to remember. In an era of conservative language, Ex-Lax was a slightly provocative but unoffensive name. Kiss was the perfect salesman, visiting drug stores to tout the benefits of the handy tablet. Timing was on his side, too, because during this period, laxatives had a reputation (undeserved, it turned out) for alleviating ailments other than just constipation.

ADVERTISING MAKES IT RUN

Over the next 20 years, the Ex-Lax tablets became a popular and effective over-the-counter medication. Matz and Kiss soon realized that "staying regular" had become an American obsession, so they decided to advertise. In 1931, they trumpeted the product with the assertion, "Your very health depends on this!" They further warned the reader that "the poisons of constipation are as real as any poisons put in a bottle!" The closing line read: "When Nature forgets, remember Ex-Lax."

NATURE'S PURIFIER

For the next ad campaign, Ex-Lax emphasized the phenolphthalein compound, claiming that the laxative was the one "that most closely approximates Nature's own way of moving the bowels." To reinforce

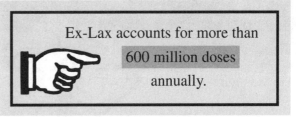

Ex-Lax accounts for more than 600 million doses annually.

these pseudo-medical benefits, Ex-Lax ads showed "real" X-rays of the intestines.

Matz and Kiss were also smart enough to know their target audience: in most cases, the mother of the household. This prompted the headline "Ask Mother. She knows!" They also offered a free sample to any mother or anyone else who wrote to the company.

When television became the dominant sales medium, the tone of Ex-Lax's advertising changed. Ads took a more genteel approach, depicting people politely mentioning that when they suffered from constipation, they took Ex-Lax for relief. The tag line was, "For regular people who sometimes aren't."

THE END

In 1981, the company was sold to Sandoz Pharmaceutical. Matz, a noted Hebrew scholar and a pioneer Zionist, had served as company president for 42 years until his death at age 81 in 1950. Kiss served even longer, as chairman and treasurer. He died in 1967 at the age of 84. Decades later, Ex-Lax can still be found in drug stores and medicine cabinets everywhere.

MALE BONDING
ELMER'S ALL-PURPOSE GLUE

STICK-TO-ITIVENESS

Gail Borden was born in upstate New York in 1801. By age 52, he had led an adventurous and varied life as a county surveyor in Indiana, a schoolteacher in Mississippi, and a newspaper editor in Texas, where he is credited with running the headline "Remember the Alamo!" But he also harbored a passion to create something useful. His first attempt was a dehydrated meat biscuit, a favorite forty-niner provision during the gold rush. Its development plunged Borden into financial ruin, although he did win an honorary membership in the London Society of Arts. To accept the honor, he journeyed to England where he met Queen Victoria. On his return voyage, Borden was distraught to see infants dying in their mothers' arms after drinking infected cow's milk. A deeply religious man, who had lost his wife and sons to yellow fever, he was moved by the suffering of strangers and vowed to find a pure, wholesome milk substitute. By 1853, he had figured out how to boil away the water in milk using an airtight vacuum. He marketed the new product as Eagle Brand Sweetened Condensed Milk.

Borden would go on to found the modern dairy industry. Eventually, the company that bore his name would develop and sell a milk-based glue whose cartoon bull would come to symbolize **Elmer's.**

MALE BONDING

SAFE AND SOUND

With financial assistance from Jeremiah Milbank, a well-known banker and wholesale grocer, Borden moved East. He incorporated as the New York Condensed Milk Company in 1858. Almost 20 years later, the company began selling fresh milk with much of its supply coming from upstate New York farms, not far from where its founder was born. In 1888, the Borden company became the first to sell milk in bottles.

Ever determined to make milk a completely safe product, Borden adhered to strict sanitary standards. He was convinced that with careful farming, a variety of milk products could be made wholesome and sustaining for American families. And thanks in part to Louis Pasteur's work in France, Borden's dream became a reality.

Gail Borden was one of the first to try to find a process for making **instant coffee** as early as 1838.

The first step was to convert mom-and-pop dairies into Borden suppliers. Next, he expanded his product line to include ice cream, cheeses, and milk powders. Single-handedly, he created public confidence in the nation's milk suppliers.

CASEIN POINT

By 1928, Borden had become a well-known and respected American dairy company, selling products nationwide. But the company searched for nonfood-based products. In 1929, it purchased the Casein Company of America, the leading manufacturer of glues made from the milk by-product casein.

MALE BONDING

After World War II, Borden's new Chemical Division sold a glue called Cascorez. But sales of the oddly named product were disappointing, so Borden decided to find a more appealing consumer name.

The Chemical Division initially planned to rename the product Elsie's Glue after the company's very popular cow. But this idea shocked Borden's Food Division, which reeled at the thought of the lovable lady bovine representing a nonfood product. A compromise was reached when it was decided that Elmer, Elsie's husband since 1951, would become the glue "spokesbull."

Elmer's was an all-purpose, adhesive product that could glue just about anything—paper, wood, leather, pottery, and almost any metal. But the real selling point was that Elmer's was nontoxic and safe for children and could be easily laundered. Sold in a convenient plastic squeeze bottle, Elmer's Glue-All became the number one seller in America. Its success led the Chemical Division to introduce an entire line (now totaling 150 items) under the Elmer name.

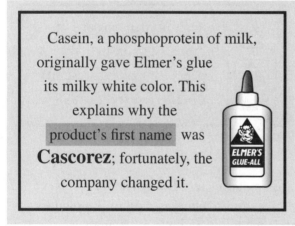

Casein, a phosphoprotein of milk, originally gave Elmer's glue its milky white color. This explains why the product's first name was **Cascorez**; fortunately, the company changed it.

BOVINE BIOGRAPHIES

n the 1930s, Borden began using a friendly cartoon heifer named Elsie as the "spokescow" for its dairy products division. At the 1939 World's Fair in Flushing Meadow, New York, the Borden exhibit's main attraction was Elsie, the first real cow many city kids had ever seen. Her stall was decorated to resemble a lady's boudoir, complete with feminine articles of clothing and accessories.

Elsie's fame soon spread to Hollywood, where she was offered a costarring role in the RKO movie *Little Men* with Jack Oakie and Kay Francis. But Elsie was in the family way, and the Borden staff members were worried about her health. To quiet their concerns, RKO provided a private railway car, a herdsman, and a veterinarian to accompany the pregnant cow on her transcontinental train ride.

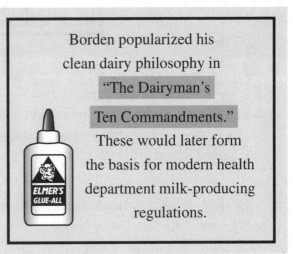

Borden popularized his clean dairy philosophy in "The Dairyman's Ten Commandments." These would later form the basis for modern health department milk-producing regulations.

Replacing Elsie at the World's Fair while she was in Hollywood posed a dilemma similar to that which had plagued Broadway producers for years: How to substitute for the famous female lead in a one-woman show? If they brought in an understudy cow who disappointed the audience, they faced a drop in attendance. On the other hand, if some ingenue cow proved more popular than the star, Elsie's popularity might decline. Borden's solution was to replace Elsie with a bull.

Overnight, Elsie's boudoir was transformed into a bachelor pad. Out went the fancy feminine frills and in came copies of *Esquire* and *The Police Gazette*. Red long johns were draped over a family portrait, and a wet towel dangled over a four-poster bed. Additional props scattered about suggested the inhabitant enjoyed a series of nightly stag poker parties. His name was Elmer. (Elmer's pedigree name was *Sybil's Dreaming Royalist.*)

MALE BONDING

THE MILKMAN'S EXIT

Elmer's Glue might not have been invented had Gail Borden not been touched by the plight of children suffering from tainted milk. Over time, the Borden company would become one of the most trusted food companies in the country. Its advertising slogan, "If it's Borden, it's got to be good" proclaimed the quality and reliability of its dairy products.

By 1870, at age 69, Borden retired, turning the operation of the company over to his sons, John and Henry Lee. In failing health, Borden prepared for his death by visiting Woodlawn Cemetery north of Manhattan, where on a shady knoll overlooking the grounds, he had a large granite milk can placed over his plot with instructions that it be removed at his burial.

He did return for one last visit to Texas to restart the meat biscuit business that had been his failing in earlier years. The factory eventually became a small town called Borden. When Borden died in 1874, his body was shipped to Woodlawn, and the milk can was removed. In its place, a simple stone reads: "I tried and failed. I tried again and again, and succeeded."

> Today teenagers drink less milk and adults consume less ice cream, and Borden's dairy business is not doing well. But *glues,* caulking, and adhesives in the non-food consumer group earned over **$2 billion in 1996.**

$AFE $EX
TROJAN CONDOMS

YOUNG'S LOVE

In 1924, Merrill Young, president of Young Rubber Company in New York City, decided to market and distribute a rubber latex condom made by a small firm in Akron, Ohio. But Young had to overcome a formidable barrier: Selling condoms across state lines was banned since contraceptive devices were prohibited by federal law. His brilliant ploy was to market the condoms for disease prevention, available only through doctors and druggists. Young's **Trojan Condoms** would later become the flash point of a Supreme Court ruling that would change forever the nation's right to access birth control products and irrevocably alter its sexual mores.

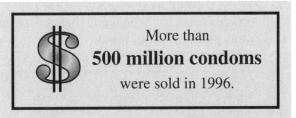

More than
500 million condoms
were sold in 1996.

CONDOM HISTORY

Although the origin of the first condom is sheathed in mystery, Egypt is generally considered the birthplace. Some theories hold that early condoms were used in the practice of a religious rite. Primitive "rubbers" were fashioned from animal membranes such as the lamb's intestine, prized for its thinness and flexibility.

$AFE $EX

Attitudes to disease prevention changed markedly after 1492 when Columbus's sailors returned to Spain with a New World scourge—syphilis. By 1493, the disease had spread via prostitution to the armies of France's King Charles VIII and, following his conquest of Naples, to Italy. This explains why, depending upon whom you want to insult, it is called the Neapolitan disease or the Spanish or French pox.

The ravages of syphilis in later centuries of the European populace led to the need for a condom that could be mass-produced. It would fall to the famous sixteenth-century Italian anatomist, Gabriello Fallopius, to invent a medicated linen sheath. In the early nineteenth century, the vulcanization process contributed to the manufacture of rubber condoms, which cost much less than those made of animal membranes.

By the middle of the nineteenth century, vulcanization offered a reliable and inexpensive way to prevent the contraction of venereal disease. But serious hurdles loomed on the horizon. Centuries of religious dogma dictated that sexual intercourse be engaged in solely for the purpose of procreation, not for making whoopee. Many religious groups viewed with outrage the easy-to-acquire contraceptive device that they believed would encourage hedonistic behavior.

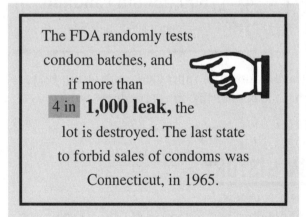

The FDA randomly tests condom batches, and if more than 4 in **1,000 leak,** the lot is destroyed. The last state to forbid sales of condoms was Connecticut, in 1965.

$AFE $EX

BIRTH CONTROL COMES OF AGE

The history of the birth control movement began inauspiciously with the 1832 publication of a pamphlet by an American, Charles Knowland, entitled *The Fruits of Philosophy*. This treatise detailed the necessity for contraception as an effective means of population control.

In the United States, Margaret Sanger would be arrested in Brooklyn in 1916 for opening a birth control clinic to distribute the diaphragm to women. Her pioneering efforts would lead to the formation of the National Birth Control League and, soon afterward, Planned Parenthood.

The conservative fabric of American society attempted to outlaw the distribution of information that even mentioned birth control. Censorship reached a climax with the passing of the Comstock Law in 1873 that directed the U.S. Post Office to cleanse the mails of obscene matter. H.L. Menken complained that because of the law it "was positively dangerous to print certain ancient and essentially decent English words." One such objectionable, decent word was "contraception."

King Charles II of England, known as "The Merry Monarch" for his many dalliances, asked a court adviser to find a method to prevent venereal disease. The adviser, the Earl of Condom, made a sheath from a sheep's intestine. And that's where we get the name **Condom.**

$AFE $EX

CONDOM CRUSADER
GIVES DRUGGIST A SQUARE DEAL

Merrill Young was so impressed with the strength of the latex condoms that he purchased the rights to manufacture them, using the Goodyear Rubber Company's double-dipped process. In 1926, he registered the Trojan brand trademark with the U.S. Patent Office.

He was savvy enough to realize that marketing contraceptives for health and disease prevention would be scrutinized by the adherents of "Comstockery" (a word coined by George Bernard Shaw). Young vigorously promoted state legislation that limited sales of rubber latex condoms to druggists in states that permitted the sale of contraceptive devices.

The Young Rubber Company became America's most well-known rubber prophylactic brand (the word condom was never mentioned). But in 1927, trouble loomed: The C.I. Lee Company of Chicago began to sell prophylactics also using the Trojan brand name. Young sued for trademark infringement in Federal Court. But, Lee's lawyers argued that since condom sales were prohibited across state lines by the Comstock Law, Young's trademark was invalid outside of New York. The U.S. District Court ruled in favor of the Lee Company.

> **Wallets** are *not* good places for keeping condoms which need a cool, dry spot at a temperature of 59° to 86°F to remain durable.

Young's successful appeal represented a landmark breakthrough for birth control proponents. The U.S. Appeals Court Judge Thomas Swan ruled that Young's purpose of marketing the condom for health reasons was legal under federal statutes and hence did not violate the Comstock Law. Further, the court ruled that

$AFE $EX

physicians could prescribe condoms for disease prevention or health enhancement, and could also inform patients about birth control. Young reaped a double bonus: He retained sole possession of the trademark and received an unpredicted boost from the advocates of birth control and contraception.

In 1933, Young polled druggists to determine whether Trojan Condoms should be nationally advertised. It was a flash point, generating national media coverage as the nation awaited the answer. The widely publicized result was a resounding, No! A Trojan ad followed, which read, ". . . such advertising is . . . unwise from an economical standpoint, indecent from an ethical standpoint, and contrary to public opinion as expressed by thinking people everywhere."

WAR TROJANS

In World War II, free Trojans were available to every GI. Some organizations complained, citing that free distribution encouraged servicemen to have sex without marriage.

Despite such product innovations as ribbed, contoured, natural lamb, and lubricated, Trojan condom sales declined by 50 percent between the years 1976 and 1986. The reasons were twofold: the widespread use of modern forms of birth control—the pill, diaphragm, spermicide, and the IUD—and antibiotics for successful treatment of venereal diseases.

Another scourge saw condom sales recover and surpass previous market totals: AIDS. According to Dr. Joyce Wallace, director of the Foundation for Research of Sexually Transmitted Diseases in New York (FROST'D), which distributes free condoms to Manhattan's streetwalkers, the incidence of HIV declined from 37 percent in 1989 to 23 percent in 1995 among prostitutes who used condoms regularly.

$AFE $EX

HIV has returned condom usage full circle—as disease prevention. Today, condoms can be found in food stores, vending machines, restaurants, movie theaters, and are easy to obtain by mail order. Credit goes to Merrill Young, who succeeded in moving the condom from the druggist's secret drawer into the bedroom.

BIG RED
HEINZ KETCHUP

HEINZ-SIGHT

In 1869, Henry John Heinz was the most lauded horseradish manufacturer in western Pennsylvania because his brand was sold in a clear glass bottle, while competitors concealed wood fiber fillers or turnip substitutes in murky green glass jars. But H.J. had always been interested in bottling other tangy sauces that Americans could add to spice up their dreary nineteenth-century diets of root vegetables, potatoes and, pickled, salted, or dried meat. He believed he could mass-market ketchup, and began to experiment with the finest grade of tomatoes, adding vinegar, salt, spices, and sweetener until he found the ideal combination. Then he packed the thick red tomato sauce in a clear narrow-necked, octagonally shaped bottle and introduced it to the public—**Heinz Ketchup**.

There are approximately *25 tomatoes* in one 14 oz. bottle of ketchup.

CATCHING UP ON KETCHUP

Many culinary experts believe ketchup was introduced by Chinese seamen in 1690, when it was called *Ke-tsiap*. As European sailors circumnavigated the globe, returning with spices, herbs, and exotic foreign dishes

BIG RED

from the Orient, one of the most popular concoctions was a purée of pickled fish found in Malaysia and Singapore. This concoction sounded to Western ears like *kechap.*

In the nineteenth century, the English retained the fish and brine base and added mushrooms, anchovies, lemons, and cucumbers, and Anglicized the spelling, adding the "t." Catsup and ketchup are different spellings for the same word, but the latter is preferred. The new mixture soon became a national favorite, a must condiment in every British pantry. Charles Dickens wrote glowingly of its flavor when the title character of his novel *Barnaby Rudge* ate with relish "lamb chops breaded with plenty of ketchup." Even Lord Byron rhapsodized about the rich and tangy sauce in his poem, "Beppo."

The critical stage of America's ketchup development occurred when Maine clipper ship captains married the newly discovered oriental fish sauce with the New World's tomatoes, the "love apples" of Mexico and the Spanish West Indies. The enterprising Maine inhabitants began to plant tomato seeds in the soil around Portland Harbor and Cape Elizabeth. They bottled the tomato sauce and enjoyed it year-round atop codfish cakes, baked beans, and all kinds of meat.

The new sauce first became popular in America when Richard Briggs, a Philadelphia printer, published *The New Art of Cookery* in 1792 with a recipe for ketchup. Isabella Beeton, the Martha Stewart of 1861, touted the exceptional taste of home-stewed tomato ketchup in *The Book of Household Management.*

When H.J. Heinz introduced his Tomato Ketchup in 1876, American women opted for the convenience of the tomato sauce in a bottle rather than slaving over an iron kettle all day. One writer praised the virtues of H.J.'s bottled ketchup as a "blessed relief for Mother."

BIG RED

Ketchup wasn't H.J.'s first success; he began by selling horseradish, pickles, sauerkraut, and vinegar. The popular new tomato sauce introduced more people to the Heinz brand name. Soon, the Pittsburgh-based firm was marketing other American standards including mustard, tomato soup, baked beans, and, finally, the first sweet pickles to be sold nationwide. (Today, a Heinz executive who remains with the company for 25 years is awarded with a pickle pin.)

Americans consume more than **1 billion** bottles of Heinz Ketchup each year.

PICKLES TO PICCALILLI

.J. Heinz is universally regarded as one of the nation's packaged foods geniuses. In the late 1880s, he took the initial steps that would shape today's multitrillion dollar food business. He presumed that most homemakers would pay retail for an item if it significantly reduced the time they had to spend in the kitchen.

In 1886, H.J. sailed to London, bringing with him seven products that were accepted by Fortnum & Mason, England's finest food purveyor. Heinz exported until 1919 when the first factory was built in the United Kingdom. The success of its soups, baked beans, and salad dressing led most Brits to believe that Heinz had always been a British institution that *exported* products to the United States.

By the twentieth century, Heinz was in practically every American household thanks to its array of foods, all sporting the distinct Pennsylvania keystone trademark label. One of the company's smarter moves was to sell kosher baked beans in its product line, appealing to Jewish families in the Northeast.

BIG RED

THE "SLOW" BOAT TO CHINA

By the mid-1960s, competition had caught up to Heinz Ketchup, which was in a battle for market share with Hunt and Del Monte; all three brands had 25 percent of the market. Heinz executives took three dramatic steps to outperform the competition: The premium retail price was lowered; the first larger-size ketchup bottle (20 ounces) was introduced; and Doyle Dane Bernbach, then the hotshot creative advertising agency, was hired to do the advertising.

On a visit to the Heinz plant, the agency's art director saw a technician conducting a viscosity test to measure the rate of flow of two ketchups side by side. As he watched the Heinz Ketchup move as slow as a glacier, while the other brand poured out of the bottle like water, the idea came to him to film the comparison. The resulting commercial proved an immediate success. Subsequent ads showed Heinz "losing the race" or being the slowest "gun" in a famous stop-motion commercial that satirized *High Noon*.

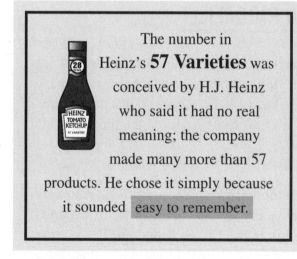

The number in Heinz's **57 Varieties** was conceived by H.J. Heinz who said it had no real meaning; the company made many more than 57 products. He chose it simply because it sounded easy to remember.

As a result of its three strategies, Heinz gained more than 50 percent of the $1 billion ketchup market, doubling its share. Heinz had raised the bar on the standard of ketchup quality to a level which other competitive brands could not reach.

BIG RED

In the 1970s and 1980s, the proliferation of fast-food hamburger chains brought the single-serve foil packets of Heinz Ketchup to millions of diners daily. Currently, Heinz is served in four out of five restaurants in the United States. Even high-class dining establishments like the 21 Club bring out the bottle of Heinz.

The rich tomato sauce that H.J. Heinz introduced in 1876 has become the second most recognizable bottle sold in America (Coca-Cola is number one). And coming full circle, the opening of American fast-food chains in China has brought the return of *Ke-tsiap* to that country after 300 years, but wrapped in the Heinz Ketchup label.

In 1941, to promote Heinz 57 Varieties, the company offered a cash prize of $25,000 to Joe Dimaggio if his consecutive game hitting streak reached 57. Fortunately for the Heinz Company, the streak was halted at 56 thanks to Ken Keltner's nimble glove.

MAKE NO MISTAKE

LIQUID PAPER

THE ERROR OF HER WAYS

n 1951, Bette Nesmith approached her first day at a new secretarial job with heart-pumping anxiety. At 27, this divorced mother of a 9-year-old son had honed her typing skills on manual machines. But now for the first time in her life, she would have to confront an electric typewriter. She watched in horror as the lightest touch spilled letters willy-nilly across the paper. The typing mistakes from a carbon ribbon would not rub off with an eraser.

Fearful of losing her job, she put some white tempera waterbase paint into a small nail polish bottle. The next day she took the bottle to the office and painted over her mistakes: **Liquid Paper.**

The original name of Liquid Paper was MISTAKE OUT.

POOLS OF TEARS AND TOIL

he story of office work in the United States chronicles a long history of women relegated to secretarial roles, where their primary function was to type business letters. For many decades before the women's movement of the 1960s, a female in an office was confined to what amounted to a gender ghetto called the typing or steno pool.

MAKE NO MISTAKE

Secretaries were required to type neat, error-free letters and documents on heavy bond paper. Typing was a manual skill, ruled by speed and efficiency. To even qualify for a position, a woman had to pass a typing test with scores measured by how many words were typed in a short period of time, minus the total number of mistakes. It didn't matter whether a woman graduated summa cum laude from Smith or Wellesley, the first question a personnel manager asked was, "How fast can you type?"

For generations of women, the fear of making too many typing errors dangled like the Sword of Damocles, hindering advancement and pay raises. Not surprisingly, it would be a woman who liberated other women from drowning in the typing pool.

Nesmith's son, Mike, was a member of **The Monkees,** a 1960's hit TV show.

TRIALS AND TRIBULATIONS

Over the next five years, Nesmith grew to depend on her little paint bottle. "Since I was correcting my own mistakes, I was quiet about it," she said. After leaving the bank job and moving on to another secretarial position, her new boss frowned upon her use of this "white-over" method. Other secretaries at work noticed Nesmith's little bottle and requested some for themselves. She began to fill a few orders, originally labeling the bottles "Mistake Out." Friends and an office supply dealer encouraged her to market the product locally. Before doing so, she changed the name to Liquid Paper, which she thought was better for a trademark, and began to experiment with improving the formula.

MAKE NO MISTAKE

In 1957, convinced that Liquid Paper had been perfected, she submitted a proposal to IBM, hoping to interest Big Blue in marketing the product. She attached two sample letters: one completed in 15 minutes using an eraser to make corrections, and a second one completed in only 2½ minutes using Liquid Paper. But IBM remained unconvinced and wanted further improvements to the formula.

In her small kitchen and garage, Nesmith continued to turn out Liquid Paper one bottle at a time with the help of her teenage son and his friends. By the end of 1957, she was selling only 100 bottles a month.

A SECRETARY'S DREAM COME TRUE

The big break came in 1958, when the trade publication *Office* listed "paper correction fluid" as one of its new products of the month. The announcement was sandwiched among descriptions of 50 other new products. Nevertheless, more than 500 readers of the magazine requested further information. One secretary who wrote in made two errors in her first sentence and joked, "As you can see, I could have used Liquid Paper for this letter."

Nesmith worked hard to fill these orders, but she never quit her day job. She toiled nights and well into the early mornings mixing and packaging the shipments. Finally, she was fired from her secretarial job for writing a letter and signing it with her own company's name. She was now on her own, head of a tiny company whose total income in a 12-month period was a paltry $1,100.

> *Secretary* magazine touted Liquid Paper as "the *answer* to every secretary's *prayer*."

MAKE NO MISTAKE

In 1962, she had to recruit part-time help as orders started to increase. A neighbor, Judy Canap, was hired to fill bottles, using plastic squeeze containers, at the rate of $.04 an item. Initially, her output totalled 500 bottles a week, but after she enlisted her husband's help, the total rose to 5,000 bottles, just the amount needed to fill Nesmith's orders!

By 1964, Nesmith married Bob Graham, who soon became her right-hand man. She began to market outside of Texas. By 1966, Liquid Paper had moved into a modernized production facility and was producing, 9,000 bottles per week.

Gillette paid *$48* million for the company in 1979 when it generated $38 million in sales.

TAKING OFF

In 1965, the small staff was housed in a portable metal building located behind Graham's house in a desolate area outside Dallas. Dan Canap remembered, "When truck drivers pulled into the driveway, they thought our business was selling portable buildings."

Liquid Paper bottles started to appear everywhere office and stationery supplies were sold. Word of mouth contributed to its success, but the one factor that accounted most for its meteoric sales rise was its visibility on thousands of secretarial desks across the country.

Eventually, Nesmith hired experienced marketing, sales, and financial experts as revenues topped $1 million for the first time in 1968. Soon after, headquarters were moved to a new building, where a fully automated line pumped out 60 bottles per minute.

MAKE NO MISTAKE

NESMITH BOWS OUT

 cottage industry operating out of a kitchen had become a $35-million-company housed in a gleaming glass building. By 1976, 25 million bottles were sold internationally, and suitors came calling. The buyer would be Gillette, which purchased the company in 1979.

Nesmith died in 1980 at age 56, leaving a fortune of $50 million, half of which went to her son and half to philanthropic foundations. One woman tired of the laborious and sloppy methods of correcting mistakes had put an end to a secretarial nightmare with a little bottle of correction fluid called Liquid Paper.

TABBY TOILET
KITTY LITTER

MODEL CLAY

After serving in the Navy in World War II, Edward Lowe returned home to manage a family-owned sawdust business in southern Michigan. Sawdust was used as an oil and grease absorbant but it was also highly flammable. To reduce the risk of a fire, Lowe substituted a less-hazardous material to soak up spills on factory floors: clay. In the winter of 1947, a customer complained that her cat's sandbox was frozen solid. She requested some sawdust, but Lowe suggested she try the kiln-dried granulated clay instead. A few days later, she returned for more of the mixture, which had delighted her tabby. Inspired, Lowe packed up 10 five-pound bags of clay granules and serendipitously hand-lettered the sacks: **Kitty Litter.**

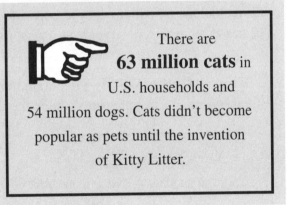

There are **63 million cats** in U.S. households and 54 million dogs. Cats didn't become popular as pets until the invention of Kitty Litter.

ALL ABOUT CATS

Cats, revered as gods by the ancient Egyptians, have been domesticated—but not always domestic—for 5,000 years. It was not the independent nature of felines that kept them out in the cold; it was their highly pungent and concentrated urine.

TABBY TOILET

For centuries, cats coexisted uneasily with humans. They were revered for killing small household vermin, but rarely invited to share hearth and home. Whereas the friendly and trainable dog would do his business outdoors, cats were impervious to behavior modification.

THE LOWE MAIN BUSINESS

From the start, Lowe sensed he had a "hot" product and travelled to nearby pet stores, selling the product from the trunk of his car.

After the initial success, Lowe travelled around the country, visiting pet stores and attending cat shows. Cat lovers thought they had died and gone to feline heaven when Lowe demonstrated how neatly and cleanly Kitty Litter worked. Like zealous missionaries, the converted convinced nonbelievers to try Kitty Litter at home. Soon, anyone with a cat in America had to have Lowe's product.

From 1947 to 1952, Lowe decorated the bags with his smiling face, and sold them primarily to pet stores under the name Kitty Litter. The first packages proclaimed: "It absorbs. Deodorizes. Takes the place of sand." By 1958, Lowe acquired a clay plant in Olmstead, Illinois, which produced 91 tons the first year, 1,700 tons the second year, and over 10,000 tons by 1960.

Lowe became so wealthy from the success of Kitty Litter that he bought 22 homes, a 72-foot yacht, a stable of quarter horses, a private railroad, and a *town in Michigan!*

TABBY TOILET

NEW MARKET RISING

As cats became popular household pets, the trend spurred the growth of cat-related items in pet stores. Prior to Kitty Litter, the pet business was dominated by canine, bird, and fish products; few cat food brands or tabby toys were sold. But with millions of cats finding a warm welcome in homes—the pet supply business exploded.

Lowe knew that cat owners tended to be as finicky as their cats when it came to buying litter products, and he wanted to ensure that his company was a step ahead in odor prevention and other litter innovations.

Edward Lowe's initial idea was that his granulated clay mixture would provide the ideal **nesting** material for **chickens.**

LOWE AND BEHOLD

Edward Lowe was a garrulous type who spent what he made, much of it on himself. As a poor child of the Depression, Lowe and his family had burned corncobs for heat and used an outhouse. Perhaps to compensate for a deprived childhood, he purchased anything and everything he wanted.

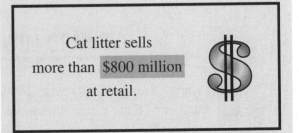

Cat litter sells more than $800 million at retail.

TABBY TOILET

But the price of his conspicuous consumption was costly for Lowe and his family. In 1984, he fired his four children and three sons-in-law in the belief that they were conspiring to take over Lowe Industries. The children and their spouses attributed his erratic behavior to alcohol abuse. When his daughters joined Alanon, Lowe said it was a ruse to help remove him from power.

Kitty Litter's inventor used **$30 million** of his money to create the Edward Lowe Foundation to help other small-business owners.

Whatever the truth, in 1985, he decided to help other small entrepreneurs by establishing the Edward Lowe Foundation, located on a 3,000-acre estate in Michigan. The organization was dedicated to educating, supporting, and representing small-business owners. The educational materials were forthright in confronting the dangers of sudden wealth.

Lowe retired from the business in 1990, after selling the company to a consortium of investors for $200 million and stock options. New capital and new management resulted in significant improvements in operating efficiency along with a new name: Golden Cat. Golden Cat reported sales of $200 million in 1994, representing the largest share of the cat filler market. In 1995, Ralston Purina, the pet food giant, acquired the assets of Golden Cat for an undisclosed sum.

EDWARD LOWE'S DEATH

Edward Lowe died in October 1995. The nation's media paid tribute to the founder of Kitty Litter, with more than 115 print obituaries, 50 television features, and 9 nationally syndicated radio segments.

TABBY TOILET

After a long and bitter estrangement from his children, Lowe renewed family ties. Over the years, he had also become an author, writing *The Man Who Discovered the Golden Cat, Reflections in the Mill Pond,* a collection of original poetry, and *Hail Entrepreneur!,* a guide to basic small-business survival skills.

One man single-handedly brought lifetimes of joy to individuals and families who now happily and cleanly share their homes with their beloved feline companions.

A PEACEFUL PERIOD

TAMPAX

A LADY'S MAN

r. Earle Haas was a family practitioner and sometimes inventor who lived in the Colorado countryside. By chance, a West Coast friend mentioned that she inserted a natural sea sponge during her period. Haas was intrigued by her resourcefulness and set out to create a product that absorbed as well as a sponge. By 1931, he would apply for a patent for a "catamenial device," borrowing from a physiological Greek term for menses. His brand name, however, was a contraction of the words tampon and vaginal pack: **Tampax.**

> Women in ancient **Egypt** were the first to fashion tampons, which they made out of *softened* **papyrus.**

THE EBB AND FLOW OF TIME

n the fifth century B.C., the noted Greek physician Hippocrates described a tampon device made from lightweight wood wrapped in lint. In Japan, they used paper. In Rome, wool. In Indonesia, vegetable fibers. In Africa, rolls of grass.

A PEACEFUL PERIOD

Later, women opted to use small homemade diaperlike external pads made of cloth, which could be reused after laundering. In 1896, Johnson & Johnson introduced a cotton external pad, but sales foundered because the company never advertised the then-taboo subject, and the product died on the shelf.

During World War I, medical inventions led to a substitute for surgical cotton: a wood-pulp derivative called alpha cellulose manufactured by Kimberly Clark Company. Nurses fashioned makeshift menstrual pads from this highly absorbent material, which worked more efficiently than cloth. When Kimberly Clark learned of the nurses' new application, it introduced a sanitary napkin in 1920 under the brand name Kotex.

THE COMFORT ZONE

D r. Haas recognized that for women to feel comfortable with a tampon he had to overcome the problems of insertion and removal. After months of experimentation, Haas used the tampon's excess cord to form a pull-string that could withdraw the device, which could then be flushed away. More difficult to overcome was women's reluctance to touch the tampon upon insertion. Haas solved that problem by encasing the tampon in an outer cylinder that delivered it directly into the vagina.

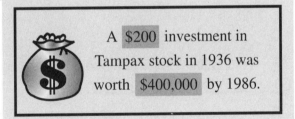

A $200 investment in Tampax stock in 1936 was worth $400,000 by 1986.

ACT I—THE PATENT YEARS

D r. Haas realized that he did not have the commercial skills to market his Tampax tampon. He sent an emissary East to interest Johnson & Johnson in his product. This seemed to be an ideal fit since J&J's home

and hospital business used similar cotton material. But when Haas's envoy arrived in New York, it was at the height of the Depression and Johnson & Johnson said no.

Help arrived when a Denver businesswoman named Gertrude Tenderich offered to buy the rights to the product. Haas sold the tampon patent and trademark for $32,000 to Tenderich and a Denver-based investment group. The sum represented a small fortune in 1933, but a decade later Dr. Haas would regret that he had taken cash and not stock.

ACT II—HERE'S GERTRUDE

German-born Gertrude Tenderich—inventor, physician, and businesswoman—must be considered the godmother of Tampax. She started producing the tampons at home using an ordinary sewing machine. Then she moved the manufacturing process to a small loft where her younger brother served as plant manager. He developed a compressor that could produce 1,100 tampons an hour.

Tenderich's efforts failed to take into account America's puritanical resistance. Rocky Mountain druggists feared that displaying the blue and white Tampax box would offend customers. Other stores refused to stock the tampons until the company advertised. This was impossible since most newspapers rejected advertising for this product.

> Some religious groups feared that Tampax would encourage ☞ **young women** to **masturbate.**

A PEACEFUL PERIOD

The energetic Tenderich was beaten but unbowed. She finally convinced the American Medical Association to accept an ad, in which women were encouraged to write for more information. She also hired registered nurses to give informational lectures about menstruation and tampons, and she mobilized crews of women to go door to door to talk to women about Tampax.

In spite of all these efforts, by 1934 sales lagged behind costs, and Tenderich was forced to license the product to the Anglo-Canadian Pulp and Paper Company of Toronto for sale in Canada and abroad. The following year, total U.S. sales had reached only $60,000. Even with the infusion of Canadian cash, the company remained undercapitalized.

Tenderich's next step was to find a partner with national drugstore sales experience. She met a sharp 45-year-old entrepreneur in New York City, a former advertising *wunderkind* named Ellery Wilson Mann whose imposing charm and marketing acumen would turn the little company into the mega Tambrands Inc.

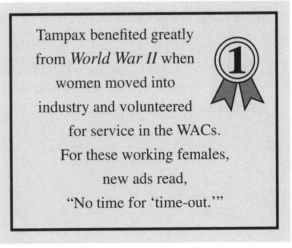

Tampax benefited greatly from *World War II* when women moved into industry and volunteered for service in the WACs. For these working females, new ads read, "No time for 'time-out.'"

A PEACEFUL PERIOD

ACT III—MANN ON THE MOVE

The date was July 26, 1936. The newspaper, the *American Weekly,* a Sunday supplement with a national circulation of 11 million. On that day, readers saw a full-page, four-color ad that heralded "Welcome This New Day for Womanhood." Boldly, it promised, "Sanitary Protection Worn Internally." The ad depicted young women dancing, playing tennis, horseback riding, and even relaxing on the beach. Mann's ad copy was clear: a modern woman could be active during menstruation.

An ensuing advertising blitz accounted for sales rising to $500,000 in 1937—the first year the company became profitable. Thirty-five years later, in 1972, sales reached $1 billion. Tampax's dominance of the tampon market—often capturing as much as 90 percent—proved to be a mixed blessing. Secure in its position, the company did little market research, and left itself vulnerable to competition by other tampon manufacturers with multiproduct lines.

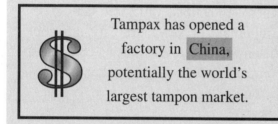

Tampax has opened a factory in China, potentially the world's largest tampon market.

Dr. Earle Haas never received monetary rewards for his invention, but in 1969, the *London Sunday Times* named him one of the "1,000 Most Important People of the Twentieth Century."

THE WRIGHT STUFF
SILLY PUTTY

A LUCKY BOUNCE

Perhaps on that fateful day in 1943 at the General Electric laboratory in New Haven, Connecticut, Scotsman James Wright was dreaming of eating haggis. While working to find a rubber substitute, he combined boric acid and silicone oil in a beaker. The result was a polymerized gooey substance. For a few seconds he stared at his new creation, and then guided by some unknown spirit, tossed it onto the floor. To his stupefaction, the material bounced back up! In 1950, a marketing expert would find the perfect name to sell this bizarre substance: **Silly Putty.**

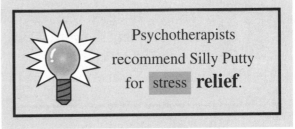

Psychotherapists recommend Silly Putty for stress **relief**.

NO PRACTICAL USE WHATSOEVER

G.E. wasn't sure what to do with Wright's goo, so they packed it off in small samples to engineers around the world requesting feedback. Replies from the world's scientific community echoed this sentiment: "This is interesting material, but we are unable to find even one functional use for it."

THE WRIGHT STUFF

Over the next four years, at G.E. and at nearby Yale University, people fooled with the peculiar material. At a cocktail party in 1949, the substance caught the attention of Ruth Fallgatter who decided to sell it in her toy store and novelty Christmas catalog.

She contacted G.E., which was happy to sell her a big lump of the stuff. Next she hired Peter Hodgson, a marketing consultant, to design and produce the catalog, which included a description of the putty. The putty was packaged in clear plastic containers, designed for women's compacts, and sold for $2.00 an ounce. The item was a big success, but Ruth Fallgatter did not recognize its full potential.

ALL HIS EGGS IN ONE BASKET

It was only Hodgson who regarded New Haven as the out-of-town tryout for the big putty show that would have to make or break it in New York City. In 1950, Peter Hodgson already had $12,000 in personal debt, but he managed to scrape together $147 to buy a batch of putty from G.E. Hodgson rejected 14 names before agreeing to Silly Putty. Ingeniously, he packed a one-ounce wad of the goo into a plastic eggshell and recommended a retail price of $1.00.

Buyers at the International Toy Fair in Manhattan doubted that children would spend a dollar on putty when they could model clay at a tenth of the price. The near-bankrupt Hodgson managed only two sales; to Niemann-Marcus in Dallas, and to

> Silly Putty has boldly gone where no toy has gone before. The astronauts on **Apollo 8** took it to the *moon* in 1968. After the voyage, Niemann-Marcus in Dallas sold the putty in commemmorative silver eggs for $75.00.

THE WRIGHT STUFF

the Doubleday bookstore chain in Manhattan. In August 1950, a writer for the *New Yorker* was browsing Doubleday's Fifth Avenue store when he noticed a salesperson playing with an egg container. Shortly thereafter, a two-page article appeared in the magazine's "The Talk of the Town" section, proclaiming Silly Putty as a unique product "that was here to stay." In the interview, Hodgson was quoted as saying, "Silly Putty means five minutes of escape from neurosis. And, as it appeals to people of superior intellect, the inherent ridiculousness of the material acts as an emotional release to hard-pressed adults."

Within three weeks after the *New Yorker* article appeared, the dumbfounded Hodgson received orders for more than a quarter-million eggs of Silly Putty! He could never have bought such publicity. Before the article ran, he averaged 10,000 eggs per month; afterward, the weekly total rose to 250,000! Interestingly, although the word "toy" was used in the article to describe the product, most of the initial consumers were adult males.

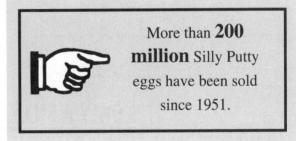

More than **200 million** Silly Putty eggs have been sold since 1951.

SALES BOUNCE THROUGH THE ROOF

It was a war that indirectly led to Silly Putty's creation and, ironically, it would be another war that almost caused its demise. When the U.S. government placed restrictions on many raw materials needed for the Korean War, silicone was on the list. At the time, Hodgson had only 1,500 pounds of the material, enough for 240,000 eggs. For a while, he had to parcel out Silly Putty, filling partial orders, and placing others on backlog status.

THE WRIGHT STUFF

Luckily in 1952, the government lifted its silicone restrictions, and Hodgson was back in business. Sales continued to increase at a steady rate for the next three years, and by 1955 the market had become exclusively children, aged 6 to 12. By 1957, sales reached an all-time high of 7 million eggs.

Peter Hodgson, the marketing wiz who engineered the success of Silly Putty, lived on 88 wooded acres in Madison, Connecticut, overlooking Long Island Sound. He named his palatial home the Silly Putty Estate.

In 1961, at the U.S. Plastics Exposition in Moscow, Silly Putty proved to be the most popular display. The popularity of the product eventually made it a big hit all over Europe.

IT'S ONLY A SILLY PUTTY MOON

When Apollo 8 journeyed to the moon in 1968, the astronauts specifically requested to take along Silly Putty, which they planned to use to hold down weightless tools and to relieve boredom. To mark the occasion, Hodgson specially designed sterling silver egg containers.

Many athletes used Silly Putty to strengthen their grip, a regimen made popular by football Hall of Famer Baltimore Colt end Ray Barry. The putty has been used to clean typewriter keys, plug leaks, remove lint from clothing, and lift color images from comics. Several stop smoking organizations prescribe Silly Putty as the perfect tactile substitute for ex-smokers who get the urge to light up.

THE WRIGHT STUFF

In 1976, Binney & Smith acquired the rights to market and sell the brand whose sales had dropped below 5 million eggs per year. The decline was due to a slew of competitors all using "Putty" in their brand names, with the exception of something called Goofy Goo. By 1980, Silly Putty sales had slipped to below 2 million eggs.

When Silly Putty turned 40 in 1990—older than G.I. Joe, Barbie, and Slinky—Binney & Smith held a birthday party at Toy Fair complete with a 500-pound cake. A year later in 1991, the eggs were produced in a glow-in-the-dark version. Currently, 6 million eggs are sold each year, thanks to renewed interest..

Silly Putty is even in the dictionary, defined as: "a trademark for a rubbery substance of silicone and methyl alcohol, used as a plaything; it stretches, snaps apart into pieces, bounces, and shapes easily."

Peter Hodgson died in 1976. The entrepreneur had taken some seemingly useless goo, named it, and risked all to sell it. He left an estate valued at over $140 million, entirely earned from Silly Putty.

MEDICAL COVERAGE
BAND-AID

HOME IMPROVEMENT

 n 1920, cooing newlyweds Earle and Josephine Dickson settled into married life at their love nest in New Brunswick, New Jersey. Alas, the young wife was inexperienced in the kitchen and frequently burned her delicate hands or cut her dainty fingers. Her husband, a son and grandson of New England physicians, would tenderly apply gauze and adhesive to her injured hands. He decided to develop a bandage that the maladroit Josephine could easily apply in his absence. Earle took some surgical tape, rolled a pad of gauze, and added a small patch of crinoline. A husband's compassionate gift to his all-thumbs wife would become the world's handiest wound covering: **Band-Aid.**

> Over the last 75 years, Johnson & Johnson has sold more than *205 million boxes of bandages*. Band-Aid is J&J's most profitable product.

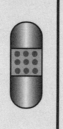

HERE'S MUD IN YOUR WOUND

 ur early ancestors learned that self-preservation depended partly upon stanching the flow of blood after injury. Mud or a mud-and-grass mixture was used to cover wounds and stop the bleeding.

MEDICAL COVERAGE

To create a germ-free environment for wounds, Dr. Joseph Lister used carbolic acid as a disinfectant in the late nineteenth century. In one of the dramatic moments in modern medicine, the English physician demonstrated the principle of anti-sepsis by ordering that all the surgical rags previously used for bandaging be boiled and used again on patients.

In 1876, New Jersey businessman Robert Woods Johnson had been impressed by Lister's theory and sought to educate Americans to the dangers of infection. His then-radical idea was that a layperson could administer first aid for minor wounds or abrasions by applying sterile bandage material. His instant method would save countless lives and reduce pain and suffering. It was also the genesis of what would become one of the best-known companies in the United States: Johnson & Johnson.

 The product's most famous T.V. commercial had a Band-Aid taped to an *egg* placed in **boiling water.** The product's adhesive power became its most important competitive advantage.

ON THE CUTTING EDGE

Dickson was employed by Johnson & Johnson. When coworkers learned about his bandage creations for Josephine, they suggested he take the idea to J&J management.

The president of the company immediately recognized the potential of this unique invention, and gave the green light to manufacture the first adhesive bandages. These were made by hand in sections 3 inches wide and 18 inches long, and were protected by removable crinoline. The consumer simply cut off as much of the roll as needed. The plant's mill superintendent W. Johnson Kenyon suggested the eventual trademark name of Band-Aid.

MEDICAL COVERAGE

Band-Aids were slow to catch on. To generate publicity, free samples were given to local Boy Scout troops, and one Ohio salesman dropped off a Band-Aid roll to every butcher shop in Cleveland.

The head of research at J&J firmly believed in the efficacy of the product. Dr. Frederick Kilmer had seen how large sterile bandages reduced infections. He realized that the smaller Band-Aids should be in every medicine cabinet or kitchen in America. As the editor of the Johnson & Johnson magazine *Red Cross Notes* for druggists, he began writing editorial pieces praising the Band-Aid.

The red string that opened billions of Band-Aids became obsolete because of the clever work of Stanley Mason, Jr. He developed a **"weak zone"** in the paper, making Band-Aids easier to open and less expensive to make.

Improvements over the decades resulted in bandages with aeration holes, Band-Aid wrapped singles in glassine, the Plastic Strip, and the Sheer Strip.

THE BANDAGE WARS

The competitive battle that would be waged between the Band-Aid and its competitors would be fought not over sterility, but over adhesive strength. In the 1930s, the company advertised the product's benefits as "a quicker, slicker sticker." A subsequent campaign proclaimed that the Band-Aid would stick "like a day-coach window," a reference to the recalcitrant train windows of the day. When television became the dominant advertising medium, J&J sponsored some of TV's early classics including *Cheyenne, The Donna Reed Show,* and *Gunsmoke.*

MEDICAL COVERAGE

Bauer and Black's Curad, J&J's main competitor, realized it had to carve out its own niche of the bandage market, and took aim at children. The first salvo fired was Curad's Battle Ribbon, a colored adhesive, followed by the "ouchless bandage." Band-Aid responded in turn with "Stars 'n Stripes," a red, white, and blue strip. Gradually, the kids' bandage wars resulted in animals, vehicles, and cartoon characters being printed on boxes and strips.

STORY'S END

Earle E. Dickson, the product's inventor, retired from Johnson & Johnson in 1957. He had been a vice president since 1932 and a member of the Board of Directors since 1929. A husband's gift to his wife had come to save lives and prevent infection.

IN THE CARDS

HALLMARK, INC.

GETTING CARDED

In 1891, his parents christened him Joyce after the last name of a famous Methodist minister. Bearing a female moniker probably toughened up the boy of the Nebraska plains. At age 16, he and his two older brothers began importing picture postcards from around the world that brought exotic views and tenderhearted sentiments to Midwesterners. At 18, Joyce Clyde Hall opened up a distributorship in Kansas City to sell greeting cards from other companies. Five years later, after the firm's inventory was destroyed in a fire, Hall convinced a bank to loan him start-up money, but this time, he would create his own line of cards. One of the first sentiments read: "When you get to the end of your rope, tie a knot in it, and hang on." Hall Brothers did more than hang on; they set the standard that has become synonymous for quality: **Hallmark.**

Since the 1960s, Hallmark has held the exclusive merchandising and card rights to the beloved **"Peanuts"** comic strip.

IN THE CARDS

KANSAS CITY HERE WE COME

J.C. Hall often said that the Hallmark company began in a shoebox because that is where he stored his postcards when he arrived in Kansas City in 1910. In this booming Midwest metropolis, he started a mail-order business, sending postcards on consignment to dealers, many who never paid his accompanying invoice.

Following World War I, America's middle class was rising, and an emerging status symbol was to send printed sentiments in a sealed envelope. Hall believed that there was an emerging market for more expensive valentines and Christmas cards.

The company's greeting card line expressed straightforward and unabashed sentimentality. They were written in unaffected homespun language that reflected the brothers' religious Midwestern upbringing. The early poems and homilies evoked warm feelings, and were always in good taste. J.C. Hall said, "I'd rather make 8 million good impressions than 28 million bad ones. Good taste is good business."

By 1923, Hall Brothers employed 120 people, and moved into its own plant on a site selected by closed-ballot vote among the coworkers. The brothers' philosophy—to treat each employee with respect—generated a positive relationship between management and staff.

Hallmark invites its retailers to come for training at the "Thoughtfulness University."

After a few years, J.C. Hall thought the company would gain more promotional value if the brand name was changed from "Hall Brothers Company" to "A Hallmark Card." He also realized that the traditional method of selling cards

IN THE CARDS

out of closed drawers inhibited sales. His innovative solution was called "Eye-Vision," a patented fixture for exhibiting cards in open vertical racks. Over time, these displays became the standard in stores for cards and other products.

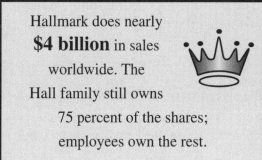

Hallmark does nearly **$4 billion** in sales worldwide. The Hall family still owns 75 percent of the shares; employees own the rest.

In 1928, the company undertook another radical step, regarded by some as "Hall's Folly." It became the first greeting card company to advertise in national magazines. In the early thirties, Hallmark sponsored a popular radio show where the host read poems and greeting card sentiments.

SENDING THE VERY BEST

On October 22, 1944, during a Hallmark-sponsored radio show, America heard for the first time one of the most well-known advertising slogans: "When you care enough to send the very best." Its creator was C.E. Goodman, a Hallmark sales vice president who believed passionately in the company's commitment to good taste and high quality.

In 1949, an in-house artist drew the memorable crown and Hallmark signature that became the company's registered trademark in 1950. In 1954, the name of the company was officially changed to Hallmark: a fourteenth-century term referring to the master craftsmanship of English guilds.

Hallmark has reinforced its quality image by sponsoring the Emmy award-winning television program the *Hallmark Hall of Fame,* which debuted on

IN THE CARDS

Christmas Eve 1951, with Gian Carlo Menotti's opera, "Amahl and the Night Visitors." For more than 45 years, this program has come to represent the highest standards in television.

UP TO DATE IN KANSAS CITY

In an effort to keep pace with modern times, Hallmark has started other card lines with more modern messages. The Shoebox subsidiary includes birthdays and get-well cards but also features themes like dating, work promotions, and other life events.

The latest innovation is called Personalize It! This line of cards enables consumers to "write their own" using an in-store computer system. And, of course, this communications giant has gone online with its own web page: *www.Hallmark.com/.*

In 1984, Hallmark acquired Binney & Smith whose product lines include Crayola, Magic Markers, and Silly Putty. In 1994, the company purchased Revell-Monogram, the world's largest maker of model kits.

Hallmark emphasizes that it has never created any national holidays, contrary to popular belief. These are deemed only by Congressional resolution. The industry-wide number of cards sold from a 1995 tally for the top three holidays are:

Christmas, 2.6 billion;
Valentine's Day, 950 million; and
Easter, 156 million.
In contrast, **Nurse's Day** generates only *500,000* card sales.

IN THE CARDS

As a family-run business, Hallmark has been a leader in addressing work/family issues. It remains one of the few American companies *never* to have laid off employees. More than a quarter of the workforce has spent 25 years working with the company.

A 1915 dream is now a decades' long reality. The Hall Brothers knew that Americans at heart were romantic sentimentalists whose eyes would grow misty at a warm birthday or Mother's Day greeting. Their little card company in Kansas City would become a multibillion dollar giant.

INDOOR SKI SENSATION
NORDICTRACK

NIGHT VISION

In 1975, Ed Pauls stared at the bleak Minnesota winter evening and rejoiced: "A perfect night for cross-country skiing." He was determined to complete hours of vigorous training for an upcoming weekend race despite the freezing rain and miserable slush. But as he plodded through the dreary night, he began to wonder why he endured the agonizing ordeal. A strange notion popped into his mind: Was it possible to cross-country ski *indoors?* He realized for this radical idea to work, a machine would have to be built that could propel a skier's body forward while keeping it in one place. Many failed models later, Pauls astounded the exercise industry with an apparatus that provided the benefits of strenuous outdoor exercise indoors. This odd-looking pulley-driven "ski" machine would work perfectly, and he would call it **NordicTrack.**

NordicTrack separates its potential market into three categories: **Enthusiast,** *Aware,* and Couch Potato.

INDOOR SKI SENSATION

ENTER THE MACHINE AGE

s recently as 30 years ago, the health and fitness industry was in the Dark Ages. By the early 1970s, the Nautilus Company debuted an array of pulley devices engineered to increase strength and improve the cardiovascular system. These machines laid the groundwork for the fitness equipment revolution.

But few people had either the room or the cash to purchase a complete Nautilus circuit. While stationary bicycles were available for indoor use, they only provided an aerobic and leg workout. For people who wanted to train at home, there existed no single apparatus designed for total body workouts.

> The original name was *Nordic Jock,* but women's groups complained about the sexist name.

FORGING AHEAD AT HOME

"Garages start great things," said Ed Pauls, and as a trained mechanical engineer, he tinkered with more purpose than most in his garage. He found the materials for the prototype NordicTrack by combing the neighborhood junkyard for special kinds of steel. He removed a flywheel belt from a piece of machinery, which he used to simulate the rocking motion used by skiers.

INDOOR SKI SENSATION

Unfortunately, his prototype was made without bars to prevent the user from toppling over—not an auspicious beginning for an apparatus designed to improve the user's health.

A second drawback was that the machine required actual cross-country skis. Users also had to put on ski boots before stepping into the skis. Regardless, Pauls donated some early models to the U.S. Ski Team for cross-training in the summer months. In 1975, word-of-mouth resulted in the sale of a few hand-constructed models.

The Paulses realized that the machine needed more exposure. They booked a booth at the 1975 Exercise Equipment Show in Washington, DC. Most of the attendees laughed at the odd-looking and expensive ($450) machine. Executives from Tunluri, the Swedish exercise bicycle company, spotted the NordicTrack and said derisively, "In Sweden, we have snow to ski on." By the end of 1975, sales totaled only 208 units.

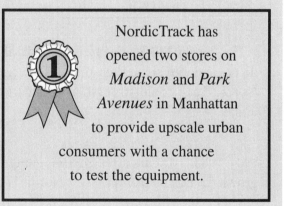

NordicTrack has opened two stores on *Madison* and *Park Avenues* in Manhattan to provide upscale urban consumers with a chance to test the equipment.

BACK ON TRACK

Ed Pauls decided to position NordicTrack as a device for total fitness workout and also for professional cross-country racing. In the late 1970s, the company benefitted from the burgeoning interest in fitness and exercise. Satisfied customers praised the NordicTrack for its aerobic and

INDOOR SKI SENSATION

anaerobic qualities, while physicians touted the health advantages of low-impact exercise. One of the first to recommend the system was their daughter, Terri, a two-time national collegiate cross-country champion. The company then struck gold when Olympic Gold Medalist Bill Koch endorsed NordicTrack.

The NordicTrack became popular in health clubs across the country. Asked years later when he realized his creation had become a success, Pauls replied, "I didn't realize how many units were going out until one day I looked out my window and saw a semi coming to pick them up. Then I was really impressed."

The Paulses employed two sales strategies: never to pressure the potential customer and to answer every health-related question. An enthusiastic staff compiled lists of new queries about physiology, weight loss, and even post-sales service.

The NordicTrack appeared at medical conventions of cardiologists, orthopedists, and physical therapists. The simple but powerful message was that NordicTrack could strengthen the heart and provide a way to exercise safely at home.

By 1985, 10 years after the first garage prototype was made, the company had grown from 3 to 80 employees. NordicTrack continued to be manufactured in two models, the standard home exerciser and the "pro" model which featured a wider base and a special resistance arm. The following year, Ed Pauls realized that he had neither the capital nor the marketing expertise to compete against larger equipment manufacturers. He sold the company to the CML Group for $24 million.

NordicTrack has sold more than 3 million sets to date.

INDOOR SKI SENSATION

THE ULTIMATE WORKOUT

The infusion of CML's new capital propelled NordicTrack into expanding markets. By 1990, 2 models grew into 16, including a $1,200 Executive Power Chair made of black leather and designed to improve upper body strength. Other models followed: NordicFlex Gold, a strength-testing machine; FitWalk, a nonmotorized treadmill; and Easy Ski, a cross-country trainer with rigid poles for extra balance. That same year, NordicTrack opened the first of its 100 retail stores. Customers were able to test the machines first hand with the assistance of experts. By the end of 1992, with the Canadian and European expansion, sales soared to $86 million.

When the original NordicTrack patent expired in 1994, engineers at the company designed a more advanced cross-country ski machine. The new model, called the MC^2, is based on electromagnetic resistance. It could simulate movement over four distinct types of snow: regular pack, fast and slow, and wet conditions, fast and slow.

In 1996, sales totaled more than $600 million worldwide. The company never lost sight of its founder's sales strategy: educate and inform the consumer. Millionaire Ed Pauls had no regrets that he sold the company 12 years ago. He tinkers in his garage, and when he gets tired of cerebral exercises, he works out on one of his five NordicTrack machines.

THOU SHALT NOT STEAL
THE CLUB

STOLEN MOMENTS

I n western Pennsylvania in 1985, the purchase of a new four-door Cadillac sedan was a symbol of financial success. When that glorious day arrived for Jim Winner, Jr., he beamed with pride at his new car, which had all the "extras"—deluxe leather interior, state-of-the-art stereo system, and the top-of-the-line antitheft system. One evening, he was horrified to discover his new car had been stolen. Neither General Motor's best antitheft device nor a car alarm had proved effective.

FBI statistics indicate that 200,000 automobiles are stolen annually. The Club helped reduce this number by as much as 44 percent in some areas.

Later, he recalled that while serving in the Army, he prevented fellow GIs from driving off in his jeep by winding a thick metal chain through the steering wheel to the brake. This would serve as inspiration for a rod of hard steel, painted bright red: **the Club**.

THOU SHALT NOT STEAL

GRAND THEFT AUTO

C ars in modern times have become as easy to steal as cattle once were. Early on, car manufacturers failed to design adequate antitheft devices. The first significant innovation was the ignition key, introduced in 1911. It didn't take long for enterprising thieves to figure out how to bypass the ignition and hot-wire the engine. Subsequently locks were placed on doors but even this wasn't an effective safeguard.

In the mid-1970s, some car owners relied on a bulky bar that attached the steering wheel to the brake pedal. It proved moderately effective, but never generated much interest. Consumers wanted an inexpensive, easy-to-use, and proven antitheft device.

COPS AND ROBBERS

O nce the idea of "can't steer, can't steal" crystallized in his mind, Winner began the process of creating and perfecting the yet-unnamed device. Initially, he worked with an auto mechanic who made an early prototype that introduced some of the final design features—length and use of high-tempered steel.

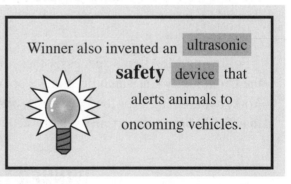

Winner also invented an ultrasonic safety device that alerts animals to oncoming vehicles.

Winner knew he needed input from car thieves and police in order to fashion the ultimate barrier against auto theft. He hired a one-time professional car thief to test each prototype. At the same time, he solicited police in Pittsburgh and Los Angeles for their suggestions. It was unanimous: the device had to be large, colorful, easy to lock, and secure. More than 50 prototypes were made and tested in high auto-theft areas.

THOU SHALT NOT STEAL

When the final version was built, Winner searched for a catchy name to describe and advertise the big, clunky rod. He thought, why not call a club a club? And so he did.

Winner worked with crime-prevention organizations like the National Fraternal Order of Police. The result of this association was called Community Carwatch, an auto-theft prevention program that brought together citizens, city officials, and local police departments. The group's goal was to educate the public on how to curb automobile theft. Pamphlets instructed participants on ways to hinder car thieves, while also recommending Winner's club.

One of the first communities to test-market the device was McAllen, Texas, where car theft had become a major problem. Initially the city planned to distribute 500 Clubs, but word-of-mouth forced them to sell or give away over 21,000! Within a month, auto theft declined 30 percent; by the end of the first year, it was down 44 percent.

Following McAllen's success, other communities signed up to participate in the Community Carwatch program. Fort Wayne, Indiana, and Irondequoit, New York, both reported car theft decreases of 40 percent after a year. Currently, more than 3,500 police departments nationwide display and demonstrate the Club.

WINNER TAKE ALL

n 1987, Winner took the Club to a Sears Roebuck buyer who was unimpressed. "Within about three minutes," said Winner later, "I was told I was out of my mind, and that my piece of metal would never sell."

THOU SHALT NOT STEAL

Winner replied, "The product will be in Sears, but you won't be the buyer." Just four months later, the nay-saying Sears buyer changed his tune when word of mouth began to circulate about the Club.

Winner proved to be the company's best and most avid salesperson. He opened accounts in retailers and auto supply chains, and kept the Club's whole-sale price the same for all outlets. "I only need the retailer for one reason, so that the consumer can easily find the Club," he said. In parking lots and on streets across America, thousands of cars sported the Club. Within five years, the device had become a household brand.

The Club sells more than $130 million annually. The company is privately held and family-owned.

JOINING THE CLUB

Today, Winner International earns more than $125 million annually thanks to the Club and other Club-type security devices. New products include the Door Club for home security, and the Bike Club, a fully adjustable, self-locking bicycle lock. And since its acquisition of the Guardian Personal Security Products Company, Winner's company also sells the Club Pepper Spray, another unique safety product. The Club's latest antitheft device is called the Shield, designed to prevent the theft of air bags.

Jim Winner purchased an empty department store in his home town of Sharon and changed it into headquarters for Winner International, Inc. This self-made millionaire operates a working Amish farm and runs a four-star country inn called Tara after the mansion in "Gone With the Wind." What else would you expect from an entrepreneurial dreamer who thinks big. Winner drives a new car and, needless to say, it's equipped with **The Club.**

THE CUTTING EDGE
CUISINART, INC.

MAN AND MACHINE

 n 1971, Carl Sontheimer, a retired electrical engineer, and holder of 52 sophisticated radar patents, attended the international housewares expo in Paris. He was captivated by a demonstration of a restaurant food processor called Robot-Coupe. Although the apparatus was bulky and unattractive, it processed fruits and vegetables in seconds. As he watched the machine gurgle and chop, he wondered if it could be reduced in size for use in American homes. Eventually, he would redesign the French machine and introduce a unique and practical apparatus: **Cuisinart.**

Cuisinart's inventor grew up in France and holds a Physics degree from MIT.

BLENDER ENDER

 he only electric machines in the typical American kitchen of the 1960s were the Waring Blender (invented by the band leader Fred Waring) and the Mixmaster, used to make cake batter and mashed potatoes. There was no machine that could knead bread dough, julienne vegetables, or grate Parmesan cheese. Dinner back then consisted of Mom's meatloaf, steak and baked

potatoes, or breaded chicken breasts, and boiled rice from a plastic bag. By the latter part of the 1970s, thanks to Julia Child, local cooking classes, and the Cuisinart, country pâtés, Coquille St. Jacques, and terrines of duck appeared on tables everywhere.

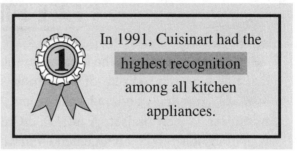

In 1991, Cuisinart had the highest recognition among all kitchen appliances.

CARL'S BAD KARMA

After he retired, Sontheimer opened a small gourmet food company called Cuisinart that specialized in importing green peppercorns packed in brine. His goal was to sell higher-priced items so he purchased the rights to make a smaller version of the Robot-Coupe. He modified the machine by lengthening the feeding tube, improving the cutting blades and disks, and adding safety features to meet American standards. He debuted this creation at the Chicago Housewares Show of 1973. When two sales reps hired to demonstrate the new food processor saw the fat, cumbersome machine with its suggested retail price of $140—four times the amount of a standard blender—they bade good-bye to Sontheimer and his Cuisinart. Retailers, too, were doubtful that even gourmet cooks would pay such an exorbitant sum for an unfamiliar, untested, and ugly machine.

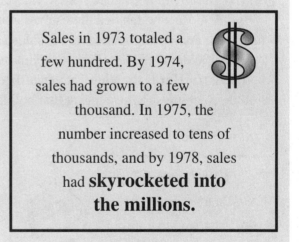

Sales in 1973 totaled a few hundred. By 1974, sales had grown to a few thousand. In 1975, the number increased to tens of thousands, and by 1978, sales had **skyrocketed into the millions.**

THE CUTTING EDGE

FREE-FOR-ALL

Undaunted after the disaster at the 1973 show, Sontheimer displayed a masterful stroke of marketing savvy by sending free Cuisinarts to America's cooking aristocracy. After they tried the machine, all were unstinting in their praise. "A hit," said Craig Calirborne of the *New York Times*. "Fabulous machine!" commented *Gourmet Magazine, Vogue, Town & Country, House & Garden,* and *House Beautiful*. But the accolade that made the biggest media splash came from the dean of American chefs, James Beard, who crowed, "This machine has changed my life. I can't live without a Cuisinart."

FAST MONEY, FAST TIMES

The explosion of interest in Cuisinart was unprecedented in the home cooking appliance industry. Everyone had to have the item, especially those who fancied themselves gourmet cooks. After reading the glowing magazine and newspaper reviews, sales soared, and Sontheimer couldn't keep up with the demand. By 1975, "Cuisinarts were moving like wildfire," remembered Larry Hurd, the chief buyer at Bloomingdale's in New York. "We had trouble stocking supplies during that holiday season."

In 1988, at age 78, Cuisinart's inventor sold his company to a group of investors for **$60 million.**

An ancillary of the Cuisinart benefit was the considerable time savings. The processor made it a cinch to chop and shred pounds of vegetables; or mix eggs into a puff shell dough in 15 seconds instead of 15 minutes.

THE CUTTING EDGE

BACK TO THE FUTURE

R obot-Coupe executives were amazed by Cuisinart's astounding success, which in their minds stemmed from their own machine. In 1980, the French company entered the American market with its own high-end food processor, proclaiming that "It *used* to be pronounced Cuisinart." This mild barb failed to sway Cuisinart's loyal following.

Carl Sontheimer made millions of dollars from Cuisinart. Even as a spry octogenarian, he marvelled that, somewhere in America, some-one was whirring, chopping, grating, and slicing food to make nut butters, flavored spreads, or pastries in a Cuisinart.

Thanks to a brilliant promotional coup conceived by the inventor's wife, at Christmas Cuisinart sold **empty boxes** containing notecards, entitling the recipient to a Cuisinart in February's shipment. That Christmas, customers were happy to pay retail for an *IOU!*

WONDER JELLY

VASELINE

OIL AND WATER

In 1859, near Titusville, Pennsylvania, one of the country's earliest drilling rigs punched a hole in the bedrock, releasing a black liquid that would forever change history. America's first oil strike became a magnet for every adventurer bent on getting rich quick. Into this boom town bedlam entered Robert Chesebrough, a studious chemist from Brooklyn, New York. He watched as a worker cleaned an oil-rig pump to remove the black residue called "rod wax," considered a nearly worthless by-product. Chesebrough attempted to extract something useful from the black gunk and finally succeeded in reducing it to a moist white jelly. Looking for a descriptive name, this lover of languages combined the German word for water *(wasser)* with the Greek word for olive oil *(elaion)* to make **Vaseline.**

The only successful product spin-off of Vaseline was **Vaseline Hair Tonic,** introduced in 1916. It gave millions of men what competitors disdainfully called the "greasy" look.

WONDER JELLY

SALVE—ATION

In the nineteenth century, the few existing medicinal remedies were based on the principles of homeopathy, which utilized the healing properties of plants and herbs. Three of the best-known salves and balms for cuts and bruises were calendula; balsamicum, made from the plant *balsamicum peruvium;* and the bright orange flower found high in the Alps, *arnica montana.* These herbal remedies were neither produced in quantity nor readily available year-round to the American consumer. Clearly, there was a need for an inexpensive healing ointment. Enter Vaseline.

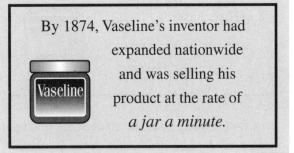

By 1874, Vaseline's inventor had expanded nationwide and was selling his product at the rate of *a jar a minute.*

Before the world would accept Chesebrough's wonder jelly, he had to convince a skeptical public that the residue gunk—even blanched a pristine white—had any salubrious effects. He also had to allay fears that this oil by-product was not combustible.

FIRST CUT

Chesebrough took two steps to overcome the resistance of doctors and apothecaries who had rejected his product. The first was to hire teams of salesmen, traveling by horse and buggy to hand out free samples to upstate New Yorkers. The second was more dramatic: He would cut and burn himself to demonstrate the effectiveness of Vaseline.

WONDER JELLY

The free giveaways—among the first of such promotions in America—generated so much interest that consumers requested Vaseline from their druggists. The prestigious British medical publication *Lancet* gave it a favorable review. In 1878, the product was a smash hit at the well-attended Paris Exposition.

One of the odder uses of Vaseline is by fishermen, who apply it to hooks to **attract trout.**

Soon the medical profession discovered the jelly's benefit, and doctors advised patients to use it for minor burns and abrasions. Other uses were to replace mustard plaster for chest colds and to relieve nasal congestion. It was universally hailed as an aid for skin- and lip-chapping. In fact, throughout the decade of the 1880s, Vaseline Petroleum Jelly was considered the handiest thing in the house.

THE PERFECT COVER

When Vaseline was introduced in 1859, it was still years before Louis Pasteur would prove that microscopic organisms called bacteria caused infection. Although unrealized at the time, Vaseline proved effective because the ointment coated cuts, preventing bacteria from reaching the wound.

Over time, physicians learned that it had no effect on the blistering process of burns, nor in fact did it contain any curative medicinal properties. Consequently, the label on today's product only claims to be a "proven moisturizer."

WONDER JELLY

TO THE RESCUE

It would be years before Vaseline's limitations would be realized, and only after it was widely used and universally praised. In the tragic 1912 Equitable Life Insurance Society fire in New York City, Vaseline treated the many burn victims. And in 1942, Vaseline was used after the Coconut Grove Night Club fire in Boston. During World War II, the Department of Defense commissioned the company to work with other leading surgical firms to develop a burn pad containing Vaseline for use in the armed services.

Commander Robert Peary, the famous Arctic explorer, had taken Vaseline to the North Pole because it didn't freeze even at temperatures of 40°F below. Conversely, in tropical climates, Vaseline—which never turns rancid—was the ideal ointment for skin abrasions and insect bites.

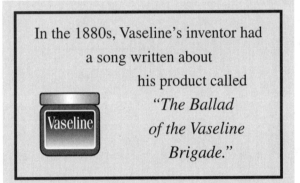

In the 1880s, Vaseline's inventor had a song written about his product called *"The Ballad of the Vaseline Brigade."*

In American households, a jar of Vaseline was kept right above the kitchen stove for emergency use on minor burns. New mothers also used it as an absorbent shield against diaper rash. No wonder the product was known as "the skin's best friend."

"POND"ERING THE FUTURE

Robert Augustus Chesebrough became a wealthy, civic-minded New Yorker known for his philanthropic works. In 1955, the Chesebrough Manufacturing Company merged with the Pond's Extract Company, founded in 1846 by Theron Pond. Wall Street called the merger the "marriage of aristocrats," as both families had been prominent in America for more than 100 years.

WONDER JELLY

When, in his mid-50s, Chesebrough suffered from a near-fatal bout of pleurisy, he insisted that he be rubbed from head to toe with Vaseline. He recovered, and lived until age 96. Near death in 1933, he attributed his long life, health, and vigor to the wonder product. He revealed publicly that for years he had eaten one spoonful of the jelly daily.

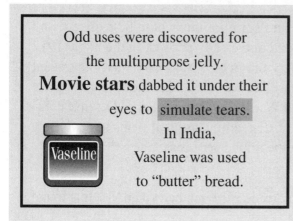

Odd uses were discovered for the multipurpose jelly. **Movie stars** dabbed it under their eyes to simulate tears. In India, Vaseline was used to "butter" bread.

SILENCE IS GOLDEN
MIDAS

SHERMAN'S MARCH

An affable traveling auto parts salesman named Nate Sherman stopped in Hartford, Wisconsin, one day in 1931 to visit a press punch operator named Joe Marx. The men talked of starting a business for themselves, and Sherman suggested selling replacement mufflers. Over the next 25 years, the team perfected a coated, rust-resistant muffler. The product went on to win the Underwriters Laboratory Seal of Approval. In the late 1940s, Sherman became intrigued by fast-food franchising and wondered if the same system could succeed in the auto parts industry. He realized that a nation-wide muffler operation would need an memorable name. He chose an acronym for his newly founded

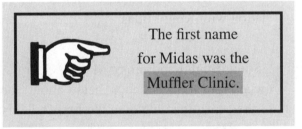

The first name for Midas was the Muffler Clinic.

dealer organization: **M**uffler **I**nstallation **D**ealers **A**ssociated **S**ervice—**MIDAS.**

THE AUTO-MAN'S EMPIRE

In the years between 1920 and 1950, the first repair garages to dot the American landscape featured "grease monkeys" in suited overalls. Often these places were a mom-and-pop service station where a trained mechanic worked on cars in a garage while Junior pumped gas. This system worked fine when automobiles were basic Model A Fords with few complex parts.

SILENCE IS GOLDEN

Post-World War II was a time of suburban boom and massive interstate road-building. The period witnessed a concomitant surge in auto production. Local service stations were unable to provide aftermarket service for the more complex V-6 and V-8 models. With millions of cars on the road, sales flourished for the Sherman/Marx line that included axles, belts, water pumps, and quality mufflers.

Midas opened a fast-food business called **Virginia Hardy Pies** that failed quickly.

SPINNING GOLD

O nce he had chosen the Midas name, Sherman, who had a flair for the flamboyant, added brass flakes to the outer coating of the mufflers. When applied, these flakes took on a golden hue and bolstered the association with King Midas.

Soon, Hugh Landrum of Macon, Georgia, a successful auto salvage dealer who owned four muffler shops, heard about Sherman's franchise concept. The result of their meeting would be the first franchise agreement. Landrum converted his operation into Midas shops and began installing mufflers at $7.00. His wife referred to the new venture as "Landrum's folly." But in short order, his four Midas stores grew to nine.

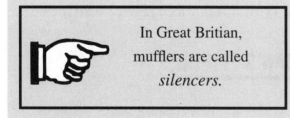

In Great Britian, mufflers are called *silencers.*

SILENCE IS GOLDEN

NATE THE GREAT

As a child in Omaha, Nebraska, Nate Sherman delivered newspapers at 3:00 A.M. to help the family pay its bills. From early on, he learned that people would work harder for something they owned. He recruited from all walks of life for his first franchises: truck drivers, oil riggers, salesmen, and mechanics. Within a year, 100 Midas locations appeared in 40 states. Sherman's franchise dream was becoming a reality.

Sherman selected the distinctive Midas typeface, dotting the logo's "i" with a majestic crown. Yellow became the color of the mechanics' uniforms, and all printed matter featured gold stamping.

Sherman knew that a salesperson's greatest asset was "getting someone to trust you." That trust was the missing component in the new enterprise. His solution was to offer consumers a promise in a simple slogan: "Midas will guarantee its mufflers for as long as you own your car."

> Midas' founder acted as a financial advisor and confidante to **Golda Meier**, Israel's former Prime Minister.

EXPANSION AND SALE

By 1965, the company had saturated the market with 500 muffler shops nationwide. Five years later, Sherman knew Midas was in need of an infusion of capital if it were to continue its growth. In 1972, IC Industries purchased the company and Sherman stepped down from day-to-day responsibilities. The new parent organization decided it was time for a new slogan.

SILENCE IS GOLDEN

CONJUGATING A NEW VERB

n ad campaign featuring one word brought Midas to the forefront of the nation's consciousness. Car owners were encouraged to "Midasize" their cars. The neologism connoted quality and reliability, and reinforced the superior workmanship of Midas dealerships.

Due to the Clean Air Act of 1975, new car mufflers lasted longer, threatening the aftermarket exhaust business. Midas repositioned itself as a complete "under-car repairs" company. By the early 1980s, it had introduced brake, suspension, and alignment services.

Midas worldwide sales topped $1 billion in 1993.

M.I.T. GRADUATES

n 1974, Sherman supervised the opening of a company research and development facility in Palatine, Illinois. He wholeheartedly approved the chosen name of M.I.T. for Midas Institute of Technology!

Nate Sherman died in 1980 at age 82. He had been a great friend to Israel, and donated large sums of money to Jewish charities.

More than *50 million* Midas mufflers have been **installed.**

Sherman's franchising concept succeeded because the muffler repair service filled a niche that local service stations could not match: a better muffler installed quickly and a lifetime guarantee.

MINI MASTER BUILDERS
LEGO

THE PLAY'S THE THING

n 1916, Ole Kirk Christiansen opened a carpentry shop in Billund, Denmark. In his off-hours, he carved wooden toys for his children. He realized he found toy-making more enjoyable and rewarding than working on big carpentry jobs. In 1934 he formed a small company, called Lego, a contraction of two Danish words (*leg godt*) that meant "play well." After World War II, Christiansen discovered the magic of plastic for manufacturing toys, and created interlocking blocks which he called Automatic Binding Bricks. Within 10 years, these sets were the company's main product and would become international favorites. By coincidence, Lego in Latin means "I put together," a fitting translation

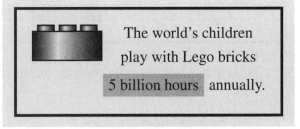

The world's children play with Lego bricks 5 billion hours annually.

since children have been assembling Christiansen's interlocking bricks with joy ever since: **Lego.**

"10"

n 1954, Christiansen sent his son Godtfred to a Danish toy fair as the representative of the Lego company, which at that time made 200 products. Godtfred met a toy buyer who complained that no multifaceted

MINI MASTER BUILDERS

toy system existed. Godtfred realized the buyer was right, and drew up a list of 10 requisites that would comprise a comprehensive system:

1. Unlimited play possibilities
2. For girls and for boys
3. Fun for all ages
4. Year-round play
5. Stimulating and absorbing play
6. Endless hours of play
7. Imagination, creativity, development
8. The more toys, the greater their value
9. Always topical
10. Safety and quality

Godtfred and his father reviewed the list to determine whether any of their 200-plus products met all 10 requirements. Only their Automatic Binding Bricks met the criteria, so in 1955, they launched the renamed product as the Lego System of Play, complete with 28 different sets and 8 vehicles. Three years later, the company perfected the stud-and-tube coupling system that allowed for unlimited combinations of bricks.

> Over *125 billion* Lego bricks have been sold since 1949.

Lego System bricks are made from high-quality plastic that is colorfast, durable, and nontoxic. All Lego pieces are fully compatible with each other. Model designs printed on the front of boxes illustrate what can be made with the pieces inside.

GREAT DANES

he success of the family-owned company started with Papa Christiansen's insistence on making quality toys. His credo was, "Only the best is good enough." To that end, Christiansen recognized the benefits of plastic in

MINI MASTER BUILDERS

the manufacture of toys. Plastic toys were durable and could be produced less expensively and in greater volume than wooden toys. Lego installed Denmark's first plastic-injection molding machine in 1947.

Godtfred was imbued with the same work ethic and vision as his father. He became the eyes and ears of the company in the European toy community, and was the first to see the marketing possibilities for inter-locking, multicolored bricks. In 1958, Lego began manufacturing its toy bricks in Germany, the same year that Ole Christiansen died.

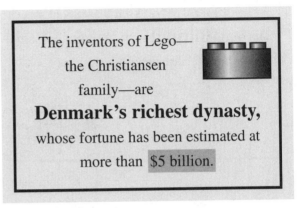

The inventors of Lego—the Christiansen family—are **Denmark's richest dynasty,** whose fortune has been estimated at more than $5 billion.

By the beginning of 1960, Lego System bricks had become the most popular toy in Europe. In 1961, they were introduced in the United States, where they were greeted with enthusiasm by children, parents, and even child psychologists. Later, many toys made in America followed the Lego 10-point play-and-use attribute system.

LANDS OF ENCHANTMENT

The Lego story could have ended with the interlocking brick system, but Godtfred had another vision: a children's theme park completely constructed of Lego bricks. In 1968, LEGOLAND Park opened on 25 acres in Billund, Denmark. Children were enchanted by miniature replicas of famous places from around the world, including the U.S. Capitol, the Greek Parthenon, and the Statue of Liberty. Even dignitaries were made of Lego bricks—Chief Sitting Bull required 1.2 million pieces. The park also features electronically controlled ships, trains, and cranes along with millions of Lego bricks scattered everywhere for young visitors to enjoy.

MINI MASTER BUILDERS

In 1996, the second LEGOLAND opened outside Windsor, England; in 1999, a third park will open in Carlsbad, California, 30 miles north of San Diego. As kids look in wonder at historical and futuristic lands magnificently constructed of Lego bricks, Ole Christiansen's wish that all children "play well" will continue to be realized.

LEGOLAND® Park in the town of **Billund** is the second most popular tourist attraction in Denmark, averaging over *1 million* visitors annually.

LET THE GAMES BEGIN
TRIVIAL PURSUIT

KNOW BUDDIES

One night in 1981, two Canadian journalists, Chris Haney and Scott Abbott, argued over who knew more trivial facts. The amicable disagreement covered topics in science, geography, and entertainment. What arose from this good-natured rivalry was the creation of the '80s must-have board game. It seemed Americans could not wait to go toe-to-toe and fact-to-fact with family and friends playing **Trivial Pursuit**.

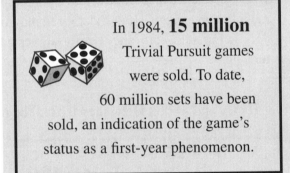

In 1984, **15 million** Trivial Pursuit games were sold. To date, 60 million sets have been sold, an indication of the game's status as a first-year phenomenon.

BATTLE OF THE BOARDS

The two board games Americans enjoyed most before 1984—excluding chess, checkers, and Mah-Jongg—were those old chestnuts Scrabble and Monopoly. The former was invented in 1931 by architect Alfred Butts, and the latter by Charles B. Darrow in 1934. In the 1970s, strategies for

LET THE GAMES BEGIN

both of these popular board games were outlined in books like *Winning at Monopoly* and *Strategies for Scrabble.* This took some of the fun out of playing and consequently their popularity declined.

Clearly, a niche existed for an adult board game that two, four, six, or more people could play. That niche would be filled by Trivial Pursuit.

AMERICAN INVASION

Haney and Abbott's first step was to outline the elements of the game; a board, cards with questions, categories, and playing icons. After deciding upon six topics (Art and Literature, Entertainment, Geography, History, Science and Nature, and Sports and Leisure), they found a small plastics manufacturer to make the six colored playing pieces. At first they named the game "Trivia Pursuit," but Haney's wife suggested "Trivial Pursuit," which sounded better.

Haney and Abbott knew they lacked the marketing, advertising, and sales skills necessary to promote the game. They convinced Haney's older brother John and attorney Ed Werner to come on board. They called the new entity Horn Abbott Ltd. (Haney's nickname was "Horn.")

> Trivial Pursuit has been translated into *19* languages and is sold in *33* countries.

Like most start-up ventures, seed money came from the partners' personal savings. Eventually the company had enough capital to manufacture 1,000 prototypes which were then sold in Ontario, Canada. The locals loved the game and found it an interesting way to pass the long Canadian winters.

LET THE GAMES BEGIN

Spurred on by their success, the team rented an exhibition booth at the 1982 International Toy Show in New York City. They were so confident that they ordered 20,000 sets. But, show buyers ordered only a few hundred games, which left the company with over 19,000 sets and the sinking feeling they might have misjudged the game's appeal.

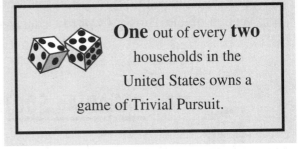

One out of every **two** households in the United States owns a game of Trivial Pursuit.

Clearly, the company needed a distribution system for the American market. They convinced manufacturer Selchow and Righter—of Scrabble and Jeopardy fame—to distribute the game in the States.

SUPPLY AND DEMAND

What ensued was an adult game-buying frenzy akin to the Cabbage Patch doll craze. As soon as Trivial Pursuit appeared in American stores, the game was snatched up—with virtually no advertising or promotion. America became obsessed with trivia, and with Trivial Pursuit.

The game succeeded for two reasons: People had fun showing off what they knew, and a nation of couch potatoes took new-found pleasure socializing around the kitchen table.

The game was designed for a wide range of interests and knowledge. Six categories with 4,800 questions had something for everyone. Mom's knowledge of soap operas and Dad's sports trivia meant they could compete with a Yale professor of immunology.

The game's fantastic success surprised the two founders, who thought they had created a pleasant board game that college graduates might enjoy—an easier version of television's *Jeopardy,* Haney said, "It's like we became rock stars."

CANADIAN SOUTHERN COMFORT

T rivial Pursuit ignited Canadian game fever. Balderdash, Scruples, MindTrap, and Pictionary were created by Canadians hoping to cash in on the revived popularity of adult board games. A Toronto bartender hit it big by inventing and selling 100,000 copies of MindTrap. In contrast, the game Orthocon, created by two friends at the University of Western Ontario, sold only 500 sets.

ல

In 1988, a scant four years after the Trivial Pursuit sales boom, Horn Abbott Ltd. sold the rights to Parker Brothers, a division of the mega toy company Hasbro, for $12 million. Parker Brothers expanded the Trivial Pursuit Master Games to include Junior, 1960s, TV, Family, and travel editions.

ல

The original Horn Abbott Ltd. team along with 32 investors who had put up $2,000 each made a big profit. Haney and Abbott became multimillionaires because the world loved to play Trivial Pursuit.

> *Today,* Haney and Abbott own *two golf courses* outside of Toronto.

IN-JEAN-IOUS

LEVI STRAUSS & COMPANY

THE OTHER GOLD RUSH

Levi Strauss was born in Buttenheim, Bavaria, in 1829, and immigrated to the United States at age 18. He began his American journey by selling dry goods in New York and Kentucky. His brother-in-law David Stern invited Strauss to be a partner in a new business venture in San Francisco, a city with a population surging from the gold rush of 1849.

A persistent myth is that Strauss cut his first pair of pants out of brown canvas tent cloth in 1853. The fact is that for 20 years he imported and sold only dry goods from his San Francisco store. It was not until 1873 when Jacob Davis, an impoverished tailor, suggested they patent a riveted waist overall that Strauss made working men's trousers. Had this new partner been more ego-centric, the world might be outfitted today in "Jacob's" and not **Levi's**.

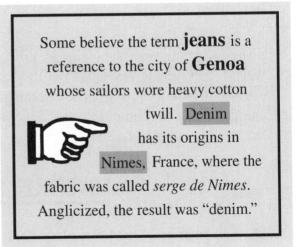

Some believe the term **jeans** is a reference to the city of **Genoa** whose sailors wore heavy cotton twill. Denim has its origins in Nimes, France, where the fabric was called *serge de Nimes*. Anglicized, the result was "denim."

IN-JEAN-IOUS

RIVETING SUCCESS

ver the next 19 years, the store prospered, moving three times to larger locations. The 1868 earthquake destroyed the enterprise, marking the first of numerous man-made and financial catastrophes that would befall the company.

In 1872, Strauss received a letter from a tailor in Nevada named Jacob Davis. His clientele, mostly miners, complained that jamming gold nuggets or rocks into their pants pockets ripped the seams. Davis's solution was to sew a line of rivets onto the pockets. He inquired whether the denim-maker would be interested in paying to register this seam strengthener. For a fee of $69 Levi Strauss & Company and Davis secured a patent for rivets, along with the now-famous double arc orange stitching in 1873.

> Levi's jeans are part of the permanent collections of the **Smithsonian** Institution.

The following year, the company produced its first pair of Patented Riveted Waist-High Overalls. A year later in 1874, it filed its first lawsuit against two competitors for manufacturing similar clothing. So great was the demand for the sturdier pants that the company opened its own factory. To run the manufacturing facility, Strauss hired Jacob Davis.

"OVERALL" SUCCESS

he primary market for Levi Strauss overalls in the last two decades of the nineteenth century was working men, especially cowboys and miners in western states. In 1880, the company generated $2.4 million in sales from both the pants and its dry goods, and became one of the most prosperous San Francisco companies.

IN-JEAN-IOUS

To reinforce its image as *the* working man's pants, Levi Strauss & Company sewed a large durable leather patch on the back of the overalls. This became the Two Horses Brand, symbolized by two stallions engaged in a tug of war over the jeans. Strauss guaranteed a free pair if they ripped.

In 1890, Strauss formally incorporated, distributing 18,000 shares of stock to family and workers. This delighted employees and was the first of many paternalistic gestures in the company's history, maintained by continuous family ownership (Strauss's four nephews worked in the business).

Levi Strauss prospered beyond his wildest dreams. He established generous scholarships for the deaf at the University of California and started the company's tradition of philanthropy. He died in 1902 at age 73.

> The company assigned lot numbers to its products in *1890*.
> The famous number *"501"* was given to the button fly trousers, which, in a memorable advertising campaign almost a 100 years later, would double company sales.

The San Francisco earthquake and fire of 1906 destroyed the company's headquarters and factory. But subsequent rebuilding would turn Levi Strauss & Company from a western working man's clothier to outfitters of the world.

NATIONAL PANTS-TIME

The reputation of Levi's overalls as "the working man's" pants was enhanced during the 1920s and 1930s. Motion pictures and newsreels from that period depicted factory workers, miners, railroad men, and cowhands wearing the familiar blue jeans.

IN-JEAN-IOUS

Ironically, the decline in family ranching in the 1930s contributed to the rise in popularity of Levi's overalls. Western ranchers, desperate to keep their spreads, converted bunkhouses to dude ranches and awaited the arrival of greenhorn easterners hungry for an authentic taste of cowboy life. These would-be cowboys had to dress the part, which meant a buckaroo outfit complete with Levi's jeans.

Hollywood played its part in moving the trousers into mainstream America. Cowboy heroes rode across the screen in Levi's. Later, in the 1950s, young film rebels like Marlon Brando made it cool to wear denims. Soon thereafter, college students in California began to wear Levi's, and by the 1960s it seemed everyone in America owned a pair of Levi's jeans.

FAMILY FORTUNES

ince Strauss had no children of his own, he hired relatives from his sister's side of the family (the Sterns) to run the company. Today, Bob Haas, the great-great-grandnephew of Levi Strauss, serves as president. In 1985, when the family grew leery of takeovers from Wall Street invaders, it borrowed $1.65 billion to buy back 95 percent of Levi's stock, effectively returning the company to private ownership. The company known for mixing profits with philanthropy continues the mission of its founder.

> The sales growth of Levi Strauss & Company is an amazing success story: $2.4 million in 1884, **$200** million in 1968, *$1* billion in 1975, $6 billion in 1996.

GET A GRIP
VELCRO

THE VELVET HOOK

In 1941, George de Mestral and his Irish Pointer were hunting game birds in the ancient Jura mountains of Switzerland. All day long, he had to pull off sticky cockleburs clinging to the dog's coat and his own trousers. De Mestral marvelled at the tenacity of these hitchhiking seedpods that were difficult to disentangle from animal fur or woolen cloth. That evening, this Swiss engineer placed a burr under a microscope and was stunned to see that the exterior of the seedpod was covered with masses of tiny hooks that acted like hundreds of grasping hands. De Mestral wondered whether it would be possible to mimic nature and create a fastener

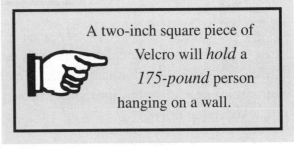

A two-inch square piece of Velcro will *hold* a *175-pound* person hanging on a wall.

for fabric. When he succeeded he gave the creation a memorable name by splicing together the first syllable of two French words: *velour* (velvet) and *crochet* (hook): **Velcro.**

A SWISS-MISS

De Mestral is quoted as saying that an inventor is "simply a madman who has a transcendent idea, a spark of light." What he witnessed under the microscope sparked his own eight-year effort to emulate the

burr-clasping system. He was so determined that, in 1952, he quit his engineer's job and convinced a Swiss banker to loan him $150,000 to perfect the Velcro concept he had patented the year before. He used part of the money to finance a trip to Lyon, the textile capital of France, where he worked with a professor. Together they experimented with nylon, a synthetic fabric that had been available since 1938. But nylon's strength created a major problem: de Mestral could not cut hooks out of the tough material. Frustrated, he recalled the warning from a close friend who had told him there were two paths to ruin for men: women and inventions, inventions being the more certain path.

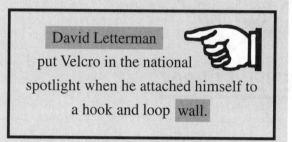

David Letterman put Velcro in the national spotlight when he attached himself to a hook and loop wall.

CAPTAIN HOOK

t age 44, de Mestral had reached a dead end and was heading to financial ruin and personal despair. With associates predicting that he would never solve the nylon-cutting problem, he returned to the mountains, vowing to return only after he figured out how to build a machine that could cut the hooked nylon fabric.

Every morning he awoke at sunrise in his small hut and considered the problem. No solution emerged. Finally, de Mestral left his alpine retreat and headed to a nearby town for inspiration. At a local barber shop, he was intrigued by the cutting and sliding motion of the barber's shears. At last he had found the answer. Velcro was back in business.

In the mid-1950s, de Mestral started production of the hook-and-loop fabric in Switzerland. He granted licensee rights with royalty agreements to companies in the United States and Canada, anticipating that the major American and European

ready-to-wear clothing manufacturers would beat a path to his door. He foresaw hundreds of uses: as replacements for zippers, laces, and buttons; and to enable aged and arthritic senior citizens and maladroit toddlers to get in and out of clothing with ease.

But Velcro suffered from a design problem. It looked as though it had been made from the left-over bits of cheap black material. Thus, when it debuted in the early 1960s, Velcro wasn't sewn into high-quality clothing. It didn't replace the laces on wing-tip shoes, the buttons on a Chanel suit, nor the zipper on designer or ready-to-wear pants or skirts.

HOW HIGH THE MOON?

S till, the invention did generate some publicity in the American scientific community. Members of the aerospace industry perceived that the hook-and-loop tape might be the ideal material for astronauts to maneuver in and out of bulky space suits. Unfortunately, the sight of spacemen in their silver Mylar suits with Velcro attachments only served to reinforce the material's seemingly limited utilitarian uses. Only the makers of children's clothing and sports apparel saw great possibilities after watching astronauts detach food pouches from walls and stand upright with their boots linked to the floor in the weightless atmosphere.

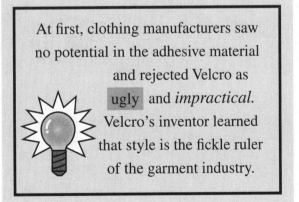

At first, clothing manufacturers saw no potential in the adhesive material and rejected Velcro as ugly and *impractical*. Velcro's inventor learned that style is the fickle ruler of the garment industry.

GET A GRIP

LET 'ER ZZZZRRRRRIPPPP

kiers packed into bulky clothing with limited mobility resembled astronauts in space suits, and sports apparel manufacturers realized that ski wear would benefit from Velcro attachments. Scuba and marine gear followed.

Velcro wallets for kids were a smash success. Book bags with hook-and-loop tape strips quickly followed. Parents and children loved the ease and independence of this wonder material.

As de Mestral had predicted, Velcro became the perfect replacement for zippers, buttons, laces, and clasps. Manufacturers found innovative uses for the material on watchbands, surgical gowns, parkas, blood pressure cuffs, even a child-safe dart board with Velcro "dart" balls.

Velcro employees are **forbidden** to use the word "Velcro," which has become a generic term similar to Kleenex and Band-Aid. They are instructed to use **"hook**-and-**loop** fastener," "hook tape," or "loop tape."

By 1978, de Mestral's patent expired and low-cost imitations from Taiwan and South Korea flooded the market, forcing Velcro USA Inc. to start an entire division just to protect the name. De Mestral began a campaign to secure lifetime copyrights for inventors.

GET A GRIP

THE HUNT GOES ON

eorge de Mestral became a millionaire from the royalties he received. He lived in an eighteenth-century chateau in the village of San Saphorin, Switzerland, 20 miles west of Lausanne.

On a trip to the Velcro USA Inc. manufacturer in Manchester, New Hampshire, de Mestral offered some advice to executives there. He said, "If any of your employees ask for a two-week holiday to go hunting, say yes." After all, one of his own hunting trips led to the invention of Velcro.

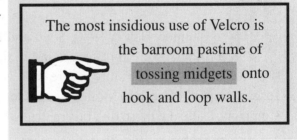

The most insidious use of Velcro is the barroom pastime of tossing midgets onto hook and loop walls.

WHEELS OF FORTUNE
ROLLERBLADES, INC.

BLADE BROTHERS

One summer day in 1980, Scott and Brennan Olson, 19- and 20-year-old brothers, were rooting around in the dusty basement of a Minneapolis sporting goods store where they worked when they came upon an old, forgotten pair of in-line skates manufactured by the Chicago Roller Skate Company. Little did these rink rats realize when they rubbed off the grime and dirt from the wizened leather boots that the genie of a billion-dollar American sporting industry would materialize and grant them a lifetime of notoriety and wealth. The Olsons' would come to name their nifty creation **Rollerblade.**

In-line skating is the fastest-growing recreational activity in the United States. Total participants climbed from 3 million in 1989 to **22.5 million** in 1995.

THE WHEELS OF HISTORY

People have been gliding on ice since the Middle Ages using wooden or metal skates. But it was not until an enterprising eighteenth-century Dutchman affixed wooden sewing spools to the soles of his shoes that

WHEELS OF FORTUNE

anyone skated on wheels. In the Netherlands, Prince James, the Duke of York, (who later returned as England's King James II), learned to skate after the Restoration. The Scots, too, got hooked on the sport and founded the first roller-skating organization, the Edinburgh Skating Club, in 1742.

In 1790, Joseph Merlin, a Belgian mechanical inventor and instrument maker, made a memorable entrance into a London masquerade party by skating in on metallic wheels that he had attached to his boots—while playing a Mozart overture on violin! Alas, Merlin was no magician when it came to stopping, and he smashed headlong into a wall-length mirror at the end of the ballroom, shattering it.

A single set of wheels set under boots came to be called in-line skates. They continued to be manufactured in Europe in the early part of the nineteenth century under such exotic names as Le Petitbled, Volito, and Le Prophete in versions made out of wood, metal, and ivory.

James L. Plimpton, a New Englander, pioneered the four-wheel skate called the Circular Running Roller Skate in 1863, made with India rubber wheels. These were the forerunner of today's modern roller skate. He also opened the first roller rink in Newport, Rhode Island, in 1866, for "educated and refined classes." The rocking-action skate immigrated to England in the 1880s, where it became such a popular activity that it coined a new term—"Rinkomania."

Roller hockey is the fastest-growing sport in America with some *4 million* participants.

Back in the United States, roller-skating enjoyed decades of popularity between the 1920s and 1950s, when roller rinks dotted the urban and rural landscapes, giving rise to a Saturday roller-skating ritual. Children and teenagers endured piped

WHEELS OF FORTUNE

organ music and rented "communal" skates that looked and smelled like . . . well, like communal roller skates.

THEY WENT ABOUT AS FAR AS THEY COULD GO

The Olson brothers purchased the patent from the Chicago Roller Skate Company. Scott would be in charge of marketing and sales, while Brennan tinkered in the workshop. They were young and enthusiastic, and Brennan was a crackerjack with tools. They headed down to their parents' basement to construct a sturdier model of the booted in-line skate. On hand were modern materials: lightweight plastic ski boots for strong support, dual steel ball bearings, and polyurethane wheels. After a few weeks and some false starts, they found the right combination and spacing for the placement of four in-line wheels. They called the invention a Rollerblade.

The Olsons demonstrated their skates by whizzing up and down the streets of their Minneapolis neighborhood. Hockey pals were impressed by the similarity to ice skating and ordered sample pairs. Soon, word spread to Nordic and alpine skiers, who adopted the Rollerblade for training.

Over forty companies manufacture in-line skates, priced from **$30** to **$600.**

Without formal business experience, the young brothers' cottage industry was doomed. By 1984, the company suffered the dual curse of many start-up ventures: insufficient capital mixed with petty squabbling. In 1985, sales had topped $300,000, but the venture was losing money. It was at this juncture they decided to sell the company.

WHEELS OF FORTUNE

THE IN-LINE MERCHANT OF VENICE

Robert Naegele, Jr., a Minneapolis financial entrepreneur, purchased Rollerblade, Inc. in 1985 for $250,000. He had a grand vision for Rollerblades: people skating atop the Great Wall of China, speeding along the canals in Amsterdam, and gliding down every street and through every park in America.

Naegele needed a splash of publicity to put in-line skates on the American Zeitgeist map. He remembered the two-mile paved boardwalk in Venice, California, where everyone flocked to gawk at bikini-clad sunbathers and weight-lifters on Muscle Beach. He recalled that the Venice walkway supported the last successful roller skate rental business in the country, *and* attracted every network television news show looking for stories on the hip California lifestyle.

In 1986, Naegele flew to Los Angeles and, shop by rental shop, *gave away* hundreds of pairs of Rollerblades. The owners were leery at first, mistaking him for a roller-skate salesman. But when he told them the deal—keep the in-line skates without charge and pocket the rental money—they realized they had nothing to lose. It took a month or two, but in-line skates caught the public's fancy. The shiny poly-urethane Rollerblades quickly displaced the roller skate as the rental of choice.

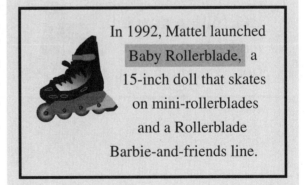

In 1992, Mattel launched Baby Rollerblade, a 15-inch doll that skates on mini-rollerblades and a Rollerblade Barbie-and-friends line.

WHEELS OF FORTUNE

BIG BUCKS AND FINAL BOWS

In 1991, demand for Rollerblades outpaced supply. To provide needed capital for expansion and research, Naegele sold 50 percent of his stock to Nordica, the ski boot giant (and a division of Benetton). He was also apprehensive of the wave of new competitors, usually low-priced imitators.

Naegele would sell his half remaining interest in Rollerblade to Nordica in 1995 for a reported $150 million. The former president of Tonka Toys was brought in to run the company in 1992, and guide it through the international expansion.

From the sale to Naegele, Scott Olson had kept a 1 percent royalty in Rollerblade. By 1997, he'll have made over $10 million from the sales. He founded Innovative Sports Systems, Inc., manufacturer of Kinetic skates and has pioneered the RowBike, a bicycle powered by the rider's arms and legs.

In-line skate sales passed **$1 billion at retail**. Rollerblade controls 50 percent of the market.

Brennan Olson continues as director of research at Rollerblade. He holds 100 skating patents and, needless to say, is a millionaire. He takes special delight in the fact that his invention has popularized a new word and sport: Rollerblading.

CLEAN SWEEP
THE DIRT DEVIL

WYSE CHOICE

In 1981, John Balch wanted to make the Royal Appliance Company a major player in the vacuum cleaning leagues ruled by Hoover and Eureka. Royal's first step had been to purchase the P.A. Geier Company, the oldest vacuum cleaner manufacturer in the United States. Balch's next step was inviting Marc Wyse, a Cleveland advertising executive, to look over Royal's line. What caught Wyse's eye was a small plastic hand-held vacuum cleaner with a mundane title: Royal Prince. He believed the machine would benefit from a better name and together with ad writer Lisa Hughes, came up with the "Bumble Bee," because the dust bag jacket resembled the shape of a bee's body. But Hughes rejected the yellow-and-black bee idea believing it was the wrong color scheme and might not sell in the housewares section of department stores. Hughes suggested painting the metal bright red. She also offered an easy-to-remember moniker for the machine, whose suction action reminded her of a small tornado: **Dirt Devil.**

> A "dirt devil" is a *tiny tornado* that often decimates crops and fields in the spring and summer.

CLEAN SWEEP

THE BIG SWEEP

he battle against dust and dirt is eternal. Primitive brooms were made of grass or reeds, and for centuries, the broom was an effective cleaning method. But when Thomas Edison demonstrated the virtues of electricity, a slew of home electrical devices followed. In 1905, P.A. Geier of Cleveland invented the first electric vacuum cleaner. These early models were upright, and used spiral brushes and beater bars which propelled dirt into reusable bags (disposable bags came years later). In the cylinder models developed after

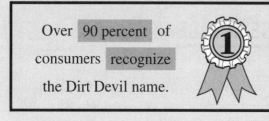

Over 90 percent of consumers recognize the Dirt Devil name.

uprights, cleaning components were mounted horizontally, allowing for greater versatility. Dirt and debris were sucked directly from the intake tube into the vacuum or dust bag.

THE DEVIL MADE HIM DO IT

At first, Balch blanched at the ad agency's suggestion of Dirt Devil. But when he perused the balance sheet of the Royal Appliance Company, he realized the company needed to gamble. Other American competitors, especially Hoover, had dominated the vacuum cleaner market for decades. (In England, Hoover's dominance is so entrenched that the verb "to hoover" means "to vacuum.")

Balch and his staff scrutinized the agency's devilish product logo design and wondered if American consumers would buy a hand vacuum cleaner named after Satan? It was time for a leap of faith.

CLEAN SWEEP

IN THE BAG

Royal advertised and promoted the Dirt Devil heavily. Balch was willing to risk all to make the Dirt Devil a household name. He expanded his distribution outlets in anticipation of demand. The company continued selling in regional department stores, then added Kmart and Wal-Mart as clients.

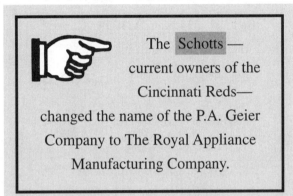

The Schotts — current owners of the Cincinnati Reds— changed the name of the P.A. Geier Company to The Royal Appliance Manufacturing Company.

The Dirt Devil performed more functions than both regular vacuum cleaners and the Dustbuster. It removed pet hairs from upholstery and carpeting, performed complete interior car care, swept trailers and small boats, and, with its long cord and powerful bristles, it was *the* handy device for dry or wet cleaning.

To attract customers, Royal encouraged stores to stack the bright red Dirt Devil boxes to form tall colonnades rising to the ceiling. Sales started to increase exponentially in 1984.

EXPANSION AND CONTRACTION

By 1991, revenues from the Dirt Devil had increased to $273 million; and net income, only $1.8 million in 1987, had jumped to $32.8 million. The company took advantage of its success and introduced other small vacuum cleaners under the Dirt Devil umbrella, including an electric broom, a lightweight upright, a power canister, and a sweeper.

CLEAN SWEEP

John Balch proved to be ingenious at promoting the company and himself. He and an adorable Golden Retriever became the stars of the company's long-running commercials for the Dirt Devil Hand Vac. He was a true believer in advertising, and spent as much as 35 percent of the marketing budget on media. So enchanted with the notion of publicity, he often told the tale of how William Wrigley, Jr., the chewing gum magnate, was on a train trip, when a friend asked Wrigley why, when his gum was already the market leader, he continued to advertise. In response Wrigley asked, "How fast do you think this train is going?" The friend answered, "About 90 miles an hour." "Well," said Wrigley, "do you suggest we unhitch the engine?"

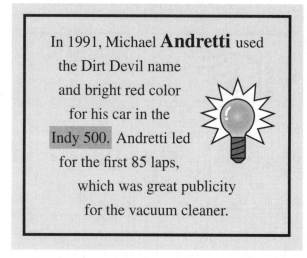

In 1991, Michael **Andretti** used the Dirt Devil name and bright red color for his car in the Indy 500. Andretti led for the first 85 laps, which was great publicity for the vacuum cleaner.

More than 10 years after taking a risk on a controversial product name and logo, Wyse and his company achieved unimagined brand recognition for the Dirt Devil.

BILLION DOLLAR DOLLY
BARBIE

THANK HEAVEN FOR THE
BUYING POWER OF LITTLE GIRLS

R uth Handler often watched her daughter Barbara play with paper dolls, while pretending they were grown-up women with exciting careers and wearing wardrobes of trendy fashions. Handler, a vice president at the Mattel toy company wondered if there was a market for a three-dimensional "older" doll. She remembered that Mattel had licensed a German doll named Lili, whose lithe figure was modeled after Brigitte Bardot. So she set to work and updated the doll's look, gave it a career and a shortened version of her daughter's name. Handler never imaged **Barbie** would become the most popular toy in the world.

> Every second *two* Barbie dolls are sold somewhere in the world.

TOY STORY

F or decades, the annual Toy Fair in New York City has been *the* place to introduce new toys for the Christmas sales season. Success at the show pays off in orders; failure at the show puts you out of business. It was at this venue in 1959 that Handler rolled the dice with her radical new creation: Barbie, the Teen-Age Fashion Model.

BILLION DOLLAR DOLLY

Not surprisingly, male toy buyers were skeptical. The slim doll with a somewhat voluptuous shape was dressed in haute couture. Barbie's wardrobe was made with genuine silk linings, miniature horn buttons, and zippers that worked. Not to mention the accessories: hats, shoes, gloves, and more. Buyers questioned whether parents would ante up for a doll whose blonde mane and provocative body seemed anything but child's play.

Even though first year sales were disappointing, Handler was certain that Barbie represented the ideal fantasy toy for young girls. She didn't have to wait long to be vindicated. Thanks in part to a television ad campaign, first year sales reached 350,000 dolls; and more important, by Barbie's first birthday, Mattel had sold more than 1 million of her costumes.

> Barbie's extensive *family tree* contains more entries than the **Windsors**— and more outfits, too.

EXPONENTIALLY YOURS

Mattel was overjoyed that Barbie had carved out a profitable segment of the doll market; in fact, the company had to double its manufacturing capacity twice within the first two years. To make her creation even more true to life, Handler decided that Barbie should resemble the girl next door with an attainable career and everyday hobbies. Although little girls loved playing fashion model, Handler acknowledged this glamorous career was beyond the reach of most youngsters.

BILLION DOLLAR DOLLY

By 1961, two years after the doll's birth, three new Barbies had been introduced: Ballerina, Registered Nurse, and American Airline Stewardess; the latter a shrewd tie-in to a recognizable company. Through the years—and continuing today—Barbie has had a succession of careers. And with each new incarnation, Barbie has shown off her new wardrobe—suits, snow parkas, sportswear, loungewear, along with a host of accessories.

With the Barbie doll craze in full swing, Handler took another creative risk: she gave Barbie a family, friends, and pets. In 1961, love interest Ken was introduced, the perfect blonde male counterpart. Little girls loved Ken and demanded even more dolls.

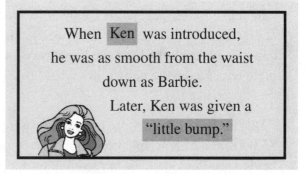

When Ken was introduced, he was as smooth from the waist down as Barbie.
Later, Ken was given a "little bump."

Midge the best friend (1963) soon appeared, followed by Skipper, Barbie's little sister (1964). Midge married Allan in 1964. Skipper made friends with Ricky and Skooter in 1965. Francie, Barbie's mod cousin (1966), was the first doll to mimic the styles of an era. And Christine (1968) was one of the first Afro-American dolls. Dancer the horse (1970) was the first of many pets.

For Mattel, the possibilities seemed endless. As women's lifestyles, wardrobes, and careers evolved through the '70s, '80s, and into the '90s, Barbie and her outfits kept pace. To date, Barbie has enjoyed more than 400 careers and had more than 500 professional makeovers.

BILLION DOLLAR DOLLY

ONE DOLL, ONE WORLD

Since that fateful day 38 years ago, Barbie has been a cash doll for Mattel, raking in over $1 billion in 1995. More than 1 billion Barbie and family member dolls have been sold in 140 countries, and a billion fashions have been designed since 1959. Worldwide sales top 1½ million Barbies per week! And her success extends beyond Mattel, to the many licensees who make Barbie accessories, consumer electronics, health and beauty aids, toys, and games. Even in today's fast-paced culture, there is Barbie as My Fair Lady complete with outfits from the Broadway musical, and Ocean Magic Barbie, complete with Keiko the baby killer whale from *Free Willy*.

Barbie has also become a collector's item. Early Barbies fetch as much as $5,000 for a doll in mint condition. Every year, more shows and conventions are held to accommodate the burgeoning retro phenomenon. In 1994, Mattel launched a Nostalgic Barbie collection and reissued the popular Enchanted Evening Barbie.

The future? Well, it shouldn't surprise anyone that Star Trek Barbie is planning "to boldly go" where no Barbie has gone before, carrying her Tricorder and Phaser aboard the Enterprise. Will this be the first outer space trip for the intrepid blonde? Not by a long shot; that was Astronaut Barbie back in 1965.

LOVIN' SPOONFUL
JELL-O

TAKE MY WIFE'S NAME, PLEASE

In 1899, Pearl Wait decided to sell his ready-to-mix gelatin business to an upstate New York neighbor named Orator Woodward. After years of tireless efforts, Wait had failed to gain a toehold on the nation's packaged foods industry. On the day of the sale, the two reminisced about Peter Cooper—the man who invented Tom Thumb, the most famous American steam locomotive of the nineteenth century. Both knew that in 1845 Cooper also had taken out the first instant gelatin dessert patent. Wait had adapted Cooper's recipe by adding fruit flavoring—like many other small gelatin companies. As the men signed the contract, Wait suggested that Woodward retain the brand name, christened by Wait's wife May: **Jell-O.**

> There are an estimated *1,800* different Jell-O *recipes.*

PEARL'S PERIL

No one is sure why Peter Cooper, an inventor of locomotives and other large mechanical devices, obtained an instant gelatin patent. In 1845, Cooper did nothing to promote the quick dessert concept, which he wrote: "Requires only the addition of hot water to dissolve it, so that it may be poured into molds, and when cold, will be fit for use."

Fifty years later, Cooper's patent came to the attention of Pearl Wait in LeRoy, New York, a prosperous town southwest of Rochester. Wait and his wife May made countless samples of Cooper's gelatin, but all tasted bland—until they experimented with fruit flavoring. May also played with the spelling of "gelatin" to invoke the term "jelly" which implied homemade and packed with fruit. She hoped the moniker would stack up against two other well-known gelatin dessert competitors: Knox and Bro-Mon Gel-On. The Waits patented the Jell-O name in 1897.

Wait had no marketing and distribution experience, so he sold the product door to door. But after two years trekking the area, he realized he had neither the time nor the capital to continue. He contacted the town's leading food manufacturer, Orator Francis Woodward, and sold the company to him for $450—enough to build a large house for his family in LeRoy.

Norman Rockwell created print ads for Jell-O in its early years.

GEL CRAZY

Orator Francis Woodward had made a fortune manufacturing plaster products: targets for trap shooting and plaster of paris eggs that kill lice when placed under chicken's nests. From his plaster business profits, he founded the Genesee Pure Food Company in 1897 with two products: a cereal called *It* that vanished virtually unnoticed and a more successful caffeine-free beverage called *Grain-O*.

In the first year, Jell-O sales were so disappointing that Woodward offered to sell the brand to the plant superintendent for $35. The employee actually refused because Jell-O had been such a sales dud. A year later in 1900, the brand would slowly begin to catch on.

LOVIN' SPOONFUL

In 1902, Woodward launched Jell-O's first advertising campaign in *Ladies Home Journal,* featuring a woman in a starched apron claiming that Jell-O was "America's Most Famous Dessert." This was the first appearance of the "Jell-O Girl," who would be a company standard until 1949. Variations on the ad always concluded with a tag line, like "You can't be a kid without it," and a reminder that Jell-O was quick and easy to prepare.

In the brand's formative years, Woodward paid handsomely to have the print ads drawn by some of the country's best illustrators, including Maxfield Parrish, Cole Phillips, Norman Rockwell, and Rose O'Neill. Later, a Jell-O children's book would be written by Frank Baum of *Wizard of Oz* fame. In 1904, when Woodward published his first recipe booklet, he was astounded that more than 250,000 were ordered. His second recipe book was published in English and five foreign languages to reach the

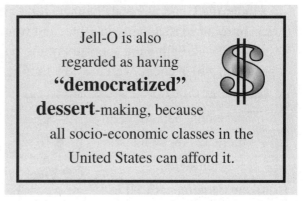

Jell-O is also regarded as having **"democratized" dessert**-making, because all socio-economic classes in the United States can afford it.

millions of immigrants thrilled to make a dessert that was advertised as "Delicate. Dainty. And Delightful."

Thanks to the ads, the recipe books, and the accessibility of the little red-and-white packages, sales topped $1 million for the first time in 1906. Grain-O was discontinued, and the company devoted all its efforts to Jell-O. Unfortunately, Wait and Woodward both died that year.

By 1923, the Genesee Pure Food Company was renamed the Jell-O Company to protect the nationally advertised trademark and to prevent the brand from becoming a generic term. Annual sales were over $65 million.

LOVIN' SPOONFUL

JELL-O'S GENERAL-IZATION

The Jell-O Company with its lucrative single-product line merged with one of Grain-O's beverage competitors, the Postum Company, makers of Grape Nuts Flakes and the popular coffee substitute Postum. This union would form the nucleus of the mega packaged goods giant called General Foods (GF).

Under the General Foods banner, Jell-O continued to prosper. Jell-O pudding was introduced regionally in 1932, and went national in 1937. For 10 years, from 1934 to 1944, both were sponsors of the popular Jack Benny Sunday night radio program, which ended with the now familiar tuneful spelling: "J-E-L-L-O." Sales of the product doubled from 1941 to 1950.

Ninety-nine percent of all Americans recognize the Jell-O name. It's in 64 percent of all U.S. homes, and sells more than *500 million* boxes per year. Every four seconds, a box is sold.

By 1957, annual production of both Jell-O products reached more than 250 million boxes. GF discontinued the LeRoy operations in 1964, when, perhaps as a symbolic end to its origins, the box was modified for the first time.

Beginning in 1970, Jell-O gelatin sales started to decline. Research indicated that women under 35, many with part-time or full-time jobs, complained Jell-O took too long to prepare. These baby boomers had been weaned on "fast" food that required little or no preparation. These women were a far cry from their mothers and grandmothers, who for more than 80 years took pride in their fancy Jell-O creations.

LOVIN' SPOONFUL

The brand that had advertised itself as "America's Red Letter Dessert" was now heading into the red. In 1987, GF hired the popular comedian and actor Bill Cosby, who since 1974 had been the pudding spokesperson, to advertise the gelatin product.

A CENTURY OF JELLO

G F also started a two-pronged strategy, directed at its older market via traditional recipe dessert marketing, while targeting the younger generation by repositioning the brand as a snack. In 1990, Jell-O Jigglers were launched. Parents could cut squiggly shapes out of a pan, and kids could eat them with their hands.

Jell-O marks its 100th anniversary in 1997, and the town of LeRoy is throwing a three-day Jell-O Jubilee. At the town's Historical Society, visitors can view old recipes, packages, and other memorabilia from gelatin's earliest years. Photographs of the Woodward family will also be on display. Tourists can drive by any of the eight houses that Pearl Wait built, monuments to the man who used someone else's recipe and his wife's ingenuity to create America's most famous dessert: Jell-O.

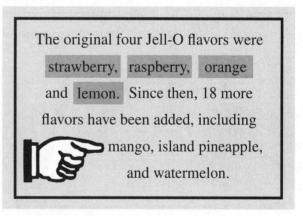

The original four Jell-O flavors were strawberry, raspberry, orange and lemon. Since then, 18 more flavors have been added, including mango, island pineapple, and watermelon.

PEN PAL
BIC

FRENCH REVOLUTION

In 1948, Marcel Bich had a revolutionary idea: an inexpensive inkwell-free ballpoint pen made of plastic. This former Italian baron who had emigrated to France had a goal to overthrow the pricey chrome and gold fountain pen. His interest in ballpoint pens was piqued when he saw American soldiers use them during the war. Although he wasn't an inventor, Bich saw the potential for a mass-produced precision writing instrument. In keeping with the eponymous pen companies of magnates Schaffer and Waterman, he would name his company after himself. Within 10 years, the future millionaire Baron Marcel Bich could say with pride, "Le stylo c'est moi" **Bic!**

> The rotating writing ball that defines a ballpoint was **patented** in *1888* by John Loud, who made *no money* from it.

POINTS OF NO RETURN

In antique shops, museums, and attics throughout the United States can be found old wooden school desks with recessed inkwells, testimony to the decades before the 1950s when the only alternatives to expensive fountain pens were cheap nibs attached to a wooden stylus. It was every kid's wish that by high school, Auntie Em would gift him or her with the much-needed fountain pen.

PEN PAL

The idea of liberating the pen from the ink bottle had long intrigued inventors. The challenge was to find a suitable internal receptacle to contain the fluid. Initially, a slender cartridge of ink was encased inside a barrel, and a spring and push-button system moved the point in and out.

These new pens with their rounded "ballpoint" tips were the source of such fascination that when Gimbels Department Store in New York City introduced a $12.50 model in 1945—an astronomical sum in that era—customers lined up just to view it.

> Daily, *15 million* Bic pens are sold.
>
> That's 5.475 billion every year.

But the ballpoints of the early 1950s were problematic since they needed to be held perpendicular to the paper for the ink to flow smoothly down. Another obstacle was that the ink often coagulated before reaching the tip. And even when the pens worked, they were messy—staining paper, fingers, and clothes.

ONE WORD: PLASTICS

Marcel Bich began making his dream a reality in the shell of an empty factory in 1945. He started a thriving business that produced parts for fountain pens and mechanical pencils. With the profits, he took two important steps toward the launching of an inexpensive ballpoint pen line: He purchased a precision Swiss machine that was capable of working metal to one-thousandth of a millimeter, and he chose plastic for his pen products.

Bich amassed a small fortune supplying European ballpoint manufacturers with empty plastic barrels, but he regarded their products as inferior. He knew he could make and market a superior pen at significantly lower cost. In 1949, he produced a long-lasting plastic pen that wrote evenly and reliably.

PEN PAL

Bich then launched an award-winning advertising campaign in France that would herald his future successes worldwide, especially in the United States. He introduced the Bic with a simple—but effective—slogan: "It runs. It runs. The Bic ballpoint." With a low-priced pen that delivered high quality, users were thrilled.

RICH BICH

Selling 42 million pens in Europe annually should have made Marcel Bich happy. But this market maven wouldn't rest until he had made it in the United States. So in 1959, he purchased the Waterman Pen Company in Seymour, Connecticut, and began an American ballpoint pen operation.

In 1953, Bic ballpoints were selling in France at the rate of *10,000 a day*. Three years later, that figure exploded to *350,000 daily*.

Research indicated that Americans were displeased with ballpoint pens available and were skeptical that anything costing 29 cents could work. Bich again turned to advertising, and created another memorable campaign. Proving the slogan, "Writes first time, every time" were "torture tests," which demonstrated how the Bic could be fired out of a rifle, strapped to an ice skate, and even driven by a jackhammer—and continue to work! Americans became converts.

THE FRENCH DEFENSE

Perhaps Marcel Bich had once cut himself using a Gillette razor. That would explain his determination to compete with Gillette's line of disposable razors and lighters, ballpoint pens, and correction fluid.

PEN PAL

The Boston-based company that King C. Gillette had commandeered to success found itself attacked on all sides by this upstart Frenchman. When Gillette introduced Cricket, the first disposable lighter, in the early 1970s, Bic challenged it with its own disposable lighter and the memorable "Flick My Bic" campaign. By the end of the decade, Gillette waved the white flag of surrender and withdrew the Cricket from the marketplace.

Bic and Gillette met again in the market war over disposable razors. The weapons were the Gillette Good News and the Bic Shavers, and they fought for this emerging segment of the throwaway razor market. Millions of promotional dollars were spent on the fray, with

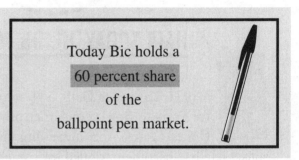

Today Bic holds a 60 percent share of the ballpoint pen market.

each company controlling about half of the market. In 1992, Bic purchased Wite-Out Products to compete with Gillette's Liquid Paper.

PEN-MAN'S SHIP

Marcel Bich became a millionaire many times over and received France's highest awards for commercial venture. His desire to succeed in the United States extended beyond the marketplace. He entered a yacht in the America's Cup 12-meter race held in Newport, Rhode Island. He would never win the event, but all who sailed against him regarded the genial baron as a true sportsman. He died in 1994, leaving behind a worldwide conglomerate that had placed Bic products in purses, pockets, and briefcases everywhere.

THE COLOR OF MONEY
CLAIROL

HAIR TODAY, HEIRS TOMORROW

In 1931, Lawrence Gelb, a New York businessman and chemist, set out for Paris to find a consumer product that could be imported into the United States. Accompanying him were his wife Joan and two young sons. Gelb had become intrigued by a small company called Mury that produced a hair-coloring preparation. Unlike other dyes that coated hair, Mury's colorant penetrated the shaft to create more natural and lasting tones. In Paris, he and his wife visited hair salons to observe the Mury product in action. They noticed that many of the women coming in for hair-coloring treatment were in their late 30s and 40s. Gelb decided that the Mury hair-coloring process was worth a $200 investment for the formula. In 1938, he secured the patent rights from the German inventor for $25,000. He kept the name, which was an adaptation of a French term for light color: **Clairol.**

Saks Fifth Avenue windows featured an array of **wigs** colored by Clairol.

THE COLOR OF MONEY

THE DYE IS CAST

The first ingredients used to change hair color came from vegetable oils, hennas, and even animal grease, although Meander, the fourth-century Athenian dramatist, wrote, "The sun's rays are the best means for lightening hair, as our men well know." Saxon men of England dyed their hair powder blue, red, green, and orange, whereas the Gauls favored reddish hair dyes, as did Queen Elizabeth whose locks were bright red.

In contrast, at the start of this century, no respectable American woman considered coloring her hair. Even in the Roaring '20s and '30s, the platinum blonde look was reserved for movie stars and showgirls. But the public's puritanical attitude toward hair-coloring did not prevent salons from offering the service clandestinely. Booths in the rear were curtained off so women could enter and exit anonymously. Due to the "underground" nature of hair-coloring, no quality control standards existed. Dyes often resulted in dull or brassy colors, and the outcome was always uncertain. Worse still was that a women could lose her hair from an adverse chemical reaction.

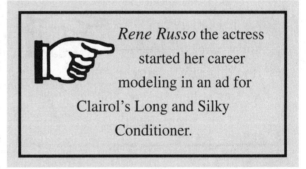

Rene Russo the actress started her career modeling in an ad for Clairol's Long and Silky Conditioner.

SALONS OF SUCCESS

Fortunately for Gelb, these salons were searching for better products for their clientele. They welcomed his French ingredients. By the end of that first year, Clairol had revenues of $80,000; sales doubled in the second year, and rose to $400,000 by the third. Gelb's wife Joan used the nom de plume

THE COLOR OF MONEY

"Joan Clair" to answer questions about the product from inquiring hairdressers. As someone who used the product, she was the ideal ambassador to tout Clairol's superiority.

Gelb wanted to establish a laboratory to develop new and better hair care products. He hired the famous Austrian biochemist Dr. Bernard Lustig to do the first early studies on hair and hair-coloring. From this laboratory, Clairol would introduce its megamillion idea of one-step, in-home hair-coloring.

A new product was created in the early 1950s called Miss Clairol Hair Color Bath. It lightened, tinted, conditioned, and shampooed the hair in a single 20-minute process. This vaulted Clairol into the home market, and enabled every woman to color her hair in privacy. But it was a different product that would usher in an era of home hair care: the Toni Home Permanent Wave.

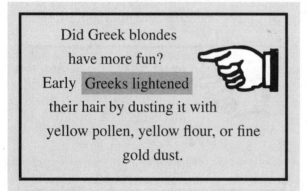

Did Greek blondes have more fun? Early Greeks lightened their hair by dusting it with yellow pollen, yellow flour, or fine gold dust.

TAKING HOME A TONI

In the late 1940s, the Toni Home Permanent Wave was launched with one of advertising's classic lines: "Which Twin Has the Toni?" Print ads showed two beautiful twins, their matching coiffures challenging the reader to guess which sister had visited the beauty parlor and which had used the Toni hair system at home.

THE COLOR OF MONEY

Clairol's rival, a hair-coloring product called Tintair ("Nature isn't always right, but Tintair is"), followed the Toni example and began to sell a hair product for home use. The company spent advertising monies profusely and succeeded in attracting new users. But Tintair could not deliver what it promised, and lasted only two years. It did, however, force Clairol management to take notice.

DOES SHE OR DOESN'T SHE?

The task confronting Shirley Polykoff, a copywriter at Foote, Cone, and Belding, was to create a print ad campaign that attracted female readers and encouraged them to buy Miss Clairol. Her now-famous line, "Does she or doesn't she?" echoed the provocative Toni question, but went further by supplying the answer: "Only her hairdresser knows for sure."

Over the years, copywriters would pen other memorable Clairol advertising lines: "If I've only one life, let me live it as a blonde!" "The closer he gets, the better you look." And the classic, "You're not getting older. You're getting better."

HEIRS APPARENT

By 1959, Bristol-Myers acquired Clairol for $22.5 million. It proved to be a savvy merger. Bristol-Myers let the Gelb family run the company autonomously, while providing wider sales and distribution for the Clairol products.

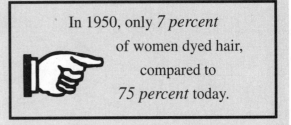

In 1950, only *7 percent* of women dyed hair, compared to *75 percent* today.

THE COLOR OF MONEY

The first successful attempt to make and market a safe hair dye was made in 1909 when a French chemist named Schuller started the French Harmless Hair Dye Company. A year later, Schuller renamed the company L'Oreal.

Clairol sales would top the $1 billion mark in 1995. The company started a successful appliance division in 1966 as well as a line of fragrance shampoos in the early 1970s. Still, the bulk of revenues continue to come from hair-coloring. Not a bad return on a $200 investment.

SOME LIKE IT HOT

TABASCO SAUCE

SALT OF THE EARTH

In 1818, Daniel Dudley Avery purchased a tract of land atop a mountain of solid salt near the Vermilion River in southern Louisiana. In 1859, Avery's daughter Eliza married Edmund McIlhenny, a bon vivant gourmand who hailed from Maryland. During the Civil War, the young couple oversaw salt production on the island before fleeing to Texas in 1863 to avoid Union troops. They returned at war's end to find the salt operation in ruins—except for one hardy vegetable crop. McIlhenny noticed that a special variety of red capsicum peppers from Mexico not only had survived but had flourished. He experimented with different pepper sauces, until he found the perfect combination of ripe red peppers, Avery Island salt, and French wine vinegar. After aging the concoction for 30 days, the mixture was strained and transferred to small narrow-necked red bottles, which were corked and dipped in green wax. McIlhenny began to sell his Avery Island seasoning sauce. To honor its heritage, he named the hot sauce after the Mexican city where the peppers had originally grown: **Tabasco Sauce.**

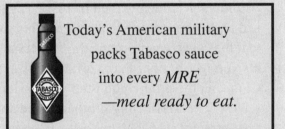

Today's American military packs Tabasco sauce into every *MRE* —*meal ready to eat.*

SOME LIKE IT HOT

POST BELLUM BOOM

In the post Civil War South, food was scarce and the piquant Tabasco Sauce spiced up bland meals. By 1868, the bottle had become so popular in Louisiana that it was referred to as "the famous sauce Mr. McIlhenny makes." The ex-banker decided to expand sales. In 1869, he sent 350 bottles to the best-known food wholesalers in the East. To his surprise, orders poured in at the staggering wholesale price of a dollar each!

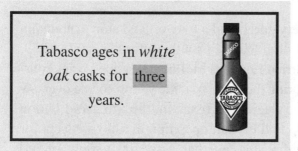

Tabasco ages in *white oak* casks for three years.

The unique formula was patented in 1870. Soon, the sauce began to appear on the tables of fine restaurants and in homes of discerning gourmets. The bright red bottle became a familiar sight, boldly advertised on thousands of barn doors throughout America.

Edmund McIlhenny died in 1890. The thriving family-owned business continued under the creative leadership of his son John who hired a theatrical troupe to tour the country performing the "Burlesque Opera of Tabasco." Several years later his younger brother Paul narrated this operatic tale to Harvard's Hasty Pudding Club, and the group requested permission to use the Tabasco name in a musical review. The McIlhenny brothers were so impressed by the club's performance they brought it to a New York City stage where free samples of Tabasco were given out.

At the outbreak of the Spanish-American War in 1898, John joined the First Volunteer Cavalry known as Teddy Roosevelt's Rough Riders and participated in the famous charge up San Juan Hill. When Alice Roosevelt, Teddy's first daughter, visited Avery Island, a white-tie dinner was held in her honor. Tables, chairs, and a statue of Lot's wife were carved out of salt.

SOME LIKE IT HOT

BLOODY MARY IS THE DRINK I LOVE

Ned Avery McIlhenny, John's son, took over in the early 1900s. During the next 30 years, Tabasco Sauce would become an international hit. In Belgium, it was used on *filet américain* (steak tartare). Italians combined it with olive oil for cooking pasta. In the Near East, Tabasco was added to falafel, tabbouleh, and sambossa. But in France, a serendipitous event would catapult sales in the United States to record-setting levels.

Fernand Periot was a bartender at Harry's New York Bar in Paris in the 1920s, a favorite watering hole of American expatriate writers, including Ernest Hemingway. Periot was the first person to mix a drink with vodka, tomato juice, salt, pepper, lemon juice, Worcestershire sauce, and cayenne pepper. Reportedly, he named this new concoction after Queen Mary Tudor of England whose executions of religious dissenters earned her the sobriquet Bloody Mary.

In 1934, noted hotelier Vincent Astor hired Periot to work in New York City's renowned King Cole Bar at the St. Regis Hotel. Astor renamed Periot's drink the "Red Snapper" thinking the original sounded too gruesome for sophisticated New Yorkers.

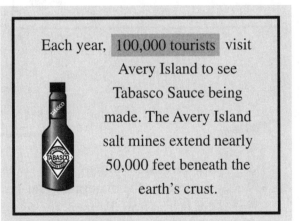

Each year, 100,000 tourists visit Avery Island to see Tabasco Sauce being made. The Avery Island salt mines extend nearly 50,000 feet beneath the earth's crust.

It was in the 1950s when bartenders discovered the Bloody Mary tasted even better with a few drops of Tabasco. Later that decade, a successful Smirnoff Vodka print campaign featuring actor George Jessel popularized the Bloody Mary. Tabasco and Sunday brunches have never been the same.

SOME LIKE IT HOT

NO CAYENNE DO

he popularity of Tabasco Sauce (outselling all other cayenne pepper products) can be traced to the amount of heat produced using only a few drops. On the Scoville Heat Unit scale, the standard meaure for heat, capsicum pepper registers over 50,000 while cayenne peppers register 30,000 units of pungency. In sauce form, Tabasco scores between 9,000 and 12,000—significantly higher than the 1,000 to 3,000 unit measure of cayenne sauces.

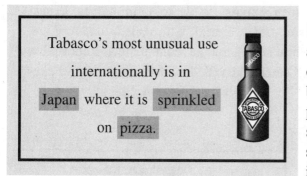

Tabasco's most unusual use internationally is in Japan where it is sprinkled on pizza.

Cooks and bartenders report that ¼ teaspoon of Tabasco is the equivalent of ¾ teaspoon of other brands of hot sauce, ½ teaspoon white or black pepper, or a pinch of cayenne pepper. And with less than 2 percent salt, the sauce is four times lower in sodium than other hot sauces—and it's Kosher.

FAMILY MAN

he current president of the Tabasco company is Edward McIlhenny Simmons, the maternal great-grandson of the founder and a biologist by profession. Peppers for the sauce are still harvested using a stick called le petit baton rouge whose bright red color indicates when peppers are ripe. Because of the enormous demand for Tabasco, 90 percent of the peppers used in the sauce are imported from Central and South America.

SOME LIKE IT HOT

Avery Island welcomes more than 100,000 visitors each year. They come to see the lush native flora in Jungle Gardens and to marvel at a 35-acre pond called "Bird City" where migrating egrets and herons roost. Many visit the Tabasco Country Store where Tabasco products, including hot sauces, seasoned condiments, and gift items are in plentiful supply. Of course, the best selling item is a bottle of "the famous sauce that Mr. McIlhenny makes."

The well-known Field Marshall *Lord Kitchener* carried a bottle of Tabasco Sauce to Khartoum, Africa, in the war against native tribes that was made famous in the movie *Four Feathers.*

The most unusual Tabasco cookbooks are **The Charley Ration Cookbook** and *No Food is Too Good for the Man Up Front.*

SPRING FEVER
SLINKY

TOY STORY

After Richard James graduated from Penn State with a degree in mechanical engineering, he went to work at the Cramp Shipyard in Philadelphia. It was World War II and his assignment was to test the horsepower of battleships using a measuring device called a torsion meter. One day, the sudden and unexpected lurch of a navy ship caused a torsion spring to fall off the table and tumble end over end across the floor. James picked it up and thought it would make a good child's toy. For the next two years, James experimented with different grades of wire and wire tension until he had perfected a combination that enabled the spring to "walk." He then asked his wife Betty to name the curious slithering apparatus. She thumbed through a dictionary looking for the perfect name to describe the action of the wire. One word stood out: Its definition read: "sleek and sinuous in movement": **Slinky.**

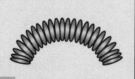

The manufacture of Slinkys has required 50,000 tons or 3,030,000 miles of wire.

SPRING FEVER

GIMBEL'S DOESN'T TELL MACY'S

After patenting the device in 1945, the Jameses borrowed $500 to pay a local company to manufacture 400 prototypes. The wire invention was a hard sell. As Betty James later commented, "A Slinky sitting on the shelf isn't awfully inspiring . . . it's kind of like a blob."

They realized that an in-store demonstration was needed to capture the toy's spirit. But, as first-time toy makers, the couple got the cold shoulder from Philadelphia retailers. Soon it was late November and Christmas was approaching. Without sales, the newly formed James Industries would fail. Push had come to beg and, finally, a sympathetic toy buyer at Gimbel's department store took pity and offered the couple a section of counterspace at the far end of the toy department.

On the night of their first presentation, the Jameses decided that Richard should go alone to prepare. Later, Betty and a friend would join him, act as enthusiastic shills and purchase Slinkys. When Betty and her friend entered the toy department, they saw a huge crowd of people waving dollar bills and shouting. She was sure that some other toy manufacturer had usurped Slinky's spot. But drawing closer, she spotted a harried Richard trying to accommodate the shoppers, all of whom wanted Slinkys! Betty and her companion never even had a chance to spend their money—all 400 Slinkys sold out that evening.

Slinky the **movie star** has appeared in *Other People's Money, The Inkwell,* and *Hairspray.*

SPRING FEVER

A RELIGIOUS EXPERIENCE

imbel's reordered the novelty in quantity. The Jameses then took their star to the America Toy Fair in New York City, where it was voted 1946's new toy of the year. The couple opened a small factory outside Philadelphia in Germantown, Pennsylvania.

During the 1950s, sales of the toy boomed thanks in part to successful advertising campaigns. Slinky made its debut on the *Romper Room Show* in 1946.

By the end of the decade, the couple had six children and a thriving business built around one unique product with no competition. Sales were robust and profits were mounting. But Richard had become involved with a religious sect and was making large contributions from the company's assets. Eventually, he ran off to Bolivia to join a branch of this cult.

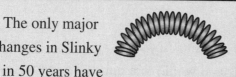

The only major changes in Slinky in 50 years have been *to coat the wire,* for durability, and crimp the ends, for safety.

NO PLACE LIKE HOME

n 1960, Betty James was left with a floundering business and six children to raise. She relocated the factory to her hometown of Hollidaysburg, Pennsylvania. The town offered her six acres on which to build a new plant, and enough friends and family to rebuild the company.

SPRING FEVER

Her next move was to hire Barton-Curteon, a small, little-known advertising agency located in Columbia, South Carolina. The agency came up with the familiar jingle, "Everybody loves the Slinky," which is still used today, more than 35 years since its first airing.

PRICE IS RIGHT

Psychologists can ponder why Slinky holds such appeal to children, but no one can argue that its low price has been a significant factor contributing to Slinky's success. In 1945, it retailed for $1.00; by 1996, the price had risen to only $2.00.

The low price was proof of Betty James's commitment to make Slinky affordable. She kept costs down and markups low. In fact, James Industries has no research and development department. Her shrewdness has discouraged competitors from bringing out a similar toy. There is almost no profit margin.

Slinkys have been used in **pecan** picking, as a **pigeon** repellent, and as **drapery** tie-backs. During the Vietnam War, Slinky was used as a makeshift radio antenna.

SPRING TIME

Slinky has transcended time and fads. Generation after generation of new parents have purchased the toy for their children. It has even been praised in *Rolling Stone*'s catalog of pop culture. And scientific journals have published articles about the properties of the slinking spring. Even astronauts on the Space Shuttle Discovery wondered whether Slinky would walk in zero gravity. It didn't.

SPRING FEVER

Over the years, Betty has refused to sell out to toy conglomerates that wanted to add the familiar item to their product lines. Today, James Industries generates more than $15 million in revenues annually.

Betty became a millionaire as well as her ex-husband, Richard, who holds the patent. Richard remarried and later died in Bolivia still devoted to the religious sect. Today, their oldest son Tom acts as sales manager, and is the only one of the six children in the business.

Slinky's 50th anniversary was announced in 1995 with the release of 400 press kits to television stations throughout the United States. Included was a T-shirt and a mahogany box containing a 14-carat gold-plated Slinky. Betty was surprised by the deluge of media requests for interviews. It seemed indeed everyone loves a Slinky!

Slinky is on display in the *Smithsonian* Institute and the *Metropolitan Museum of Art.*

RUNNING HOT AND COLD
THERMOS

VACUUM PACKED

The Scots may have lost their freedom to England, but over the years they have maintained their own monetary and educational systems, the latter which produced an outstanding group of engineers, chemists, and mathematicians. It was this system that encouraged James Dewar (1842–1923) to experiment with very low temperatures and the liquification of gases. In 1893, he hit upon the idea of placing one flask inside another which created a vacuum between them and prevented the passage of heat from one bottle to the other. As a scientist who had no interest in commercial gain, he never patented the idea. But the German firm of Burger and Aschenbrenner in Munich that had been hired to make the calibrated flasks realized that the vacuum bottle might have commercial potential. In 1904, the firm sponsored a contest to find a brand name. The winner was a Munich resident who adapted the Greek word for heat (*thérmê*) and came up with: **Thermos.**

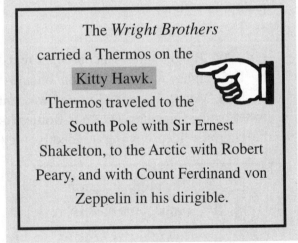

The *Wright Brothers* carried a Thermos on the Kitty Hawk. Thermos traveled to the South Pole with Sir Ernest Shakelton, to the Arctic with Robert Peary, and with Count Ferdinand von Zeppelin in his dirigible.

RUNNING HOT AND COLD

WET AND WILD

Historically, liquids have been transported in glass bottles, pitchers, jugs, ewers, even in skin bags. But all of these apparatuses lacked the ability to maintain temperature.

The Thermos bottle would solve this problem. Media attention given to the new container quickly captured the public's imagination. By 1907 the Thermos had traveled to exotic places around the globe. Photographs, most memorably of Teddy Roosevelt's trek through Africa, proved the reliability and portability of the new vacuum bottle.

Four national licensing agreements created Thermos manufacturing companies in the United Kingdom, the United States, Canada, and Japan. Each of these entities would make the Thermos according to a standard that would guarantee quality throughout the world.

In 1906, Burger and Aschenbrenner registered the Thermos name and licensed the U.S. rights to an American businessman named William Walker from Portland, Maine. Thermos Limited was founded in England that same year, followed by the Canadian Thermos Bottle Company in Montreal in 1907. In 1910, the Thermos license was extended by the Germans to Nippon Sanso in Tokyo.

The original Thermos container is on display at *London's Royal Institute.*

The Japanese were also interested in the American company product extensions, which included picnic containers, coffeepots, and decanters using Dewar's vacuum technology and the German parent's bottle-making methods.

RUNNING HOT AND COLD

By 1913, American Thermos had moved from Maine to Norwich, Connecticut, where it expanded to include lunch kits and products for the outdoors. Thermos items were even used by the laborers who built the Panama Canal.

THE END OF A BEAUTIFUL FRIENDSHIP

Thermos Limited, the British licensee, had established a factory in the London suburb of Tottenham. For years it paid the annual licensing royalty to Thermos GmbH., its German partner. Relations between the two companies were excellent; the German firm always credited Sir James Dewar as the inventor of the vacuum process, and the British always praised the German company for having the foresight to realize the product's commercial applications.

In 1914, the British Ministry of Munitions took over Thermos Limited and manufactured shell cases and other equipment for the war effort. Soon after, the management of Thermos Limited purchased the Tottenham factory outright and severed all relationship with its German parent.

In 1917, a Zeppelin bombed the Tottenham factory and destroyed it. Historians have speculated that Kaiser Wilhelm's war cabinet, tipped off by Thermos Germany, knew that more than vacuum bottles were being made at the British factory.

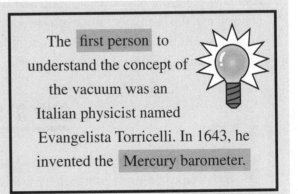

The first person to understand the concept of the vacuum was an Italian physicist named Evangelista Torricelli. In 1643, he invented the Mercury barometer.

RUNNING HOT AND COLD

COURTING DISASTER

n a landmark American case that resulted in a permanent loss of exclusive ownership of the thermos name, the Thermos company had to cede the right to use the name to its chief competitor Aladdin Industries. One attorney said of the 1962 ruling that the ". . . opinion stands as a case history of what can go wrong with a successful trademark."

The judge ruled that thermos had become a generic term for a vacuum bottle and, therefore, other companies could use the word to identify their bottles, but they were restricted to a lowercase "t." To reach his decision, the judge examined the company's advertising policies and investigations into improper trademark use. He found that the Thermos Company had contributed to making the word generic by "popularizing the expression Thermos bottle."

> It was the pint-sized *"Blue Bottle"* introduced in 1924 for $.98 that became the most famous and most used of the Thermos line.

This was not the only time a brand had to relinquish the right to a name: aspirin, cellophane, the escalator, and even shredded wheat all have become generic product terminology. But the Thermos company did retain use of the "uppercase" Thermos and all its registered trademarks.

CUP O' SOUP

he Thermos bottle became part of the American landscape. Workers and schoolchildren everywhere could be seen unscrewing Thermos bottles and pouring a piping hot cup of homemade soup or coffee.

RUNNING HOT AND COLD

Currently, Thermos products try to keep a competitive edge by expanding their product line to include grills, coolers, and vacuum bottles. Sales have grown by licensing to other companies that sell to the children's market. Recent items include lunch boxes featuring Disney characters, Barney, and the puppet Lamb Chop.

Somewhere in the world today, someone at school or at work is enjoying a cup of cold or hot nourishment by opening up the handy vacuum bottle invented by a Scotsman, patented by Germans, popularized by Americans, and named after a Greek word: Thermos.

LITTLE VITTLES
GERBER

INTO THE MOUTHS OF BABES

Dorothy Gerber was determined to give her daughter the best of everything. It was 1927 and her pediatrician espoused somewhat advanced views on infant nutrition. He recommended the feeding of strained food as early as five months. The dutiful Fremont, Michigan mother began the tiresome chore of peeling, steaming, scraping, and straining the fruits and vegetables available. But as delighted as she was with her daughter's gurgling appreciation, Gerber believed there had to be a simpler and easier way to prepare baby food.

While Gerber was certainly not the first mother in America to have this notion, she was the one to do something about it. She asked her husband, the son of the president of Fremont Canning Company, why infant foods could not be canned, too. Her husband Dan and his father Frank pondered the question. They couldn't think of any reason why baby food could not be commercially produced. So, they prepared test packs of baby food for Dorothy and for other cannery workers with babies. The response was overwhelmingly enthusiastic; the babies loved the stuff. The company decided to manufacture baby food and sell it under the name of the family that inspired it: **Gerber.**

Gerber is sold in 70 countries with labeling in 12 languages. Sales total more than **$1 billion annually.**

LITTLE VITTLES

A LOT OF LITTLE REASONS

Mothers have always fed babies minced or masticated food. The evolution of cooking enabled people to break down foods through the heating process, and set the early stages for prepared baby foods. Cooked vegetables became soft and easy to grind, and generated a broth that babies could drink.

The innovation of canned food would be the next stop on the road to commercially sold baby food. Canning came about primarily for military purposes. The French government under Napoleon offered a prize to anyone who developed a method for preserving food.

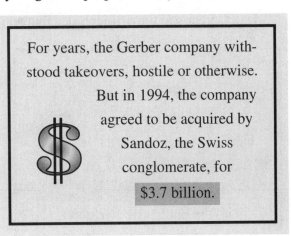

For years, the Gerber company withstood takeovers, hostile or otherwise. But in 1994, the company agreed to be acquired by Sandoz, the Swiss conglomerate, for $3.7 billion.

AND GERBER MAKES THREE

The decision to manufacture canned baby food was a daring one in 1928. The Fremont Canning Company—the name would be changed to Gerber in 1941—faced the daunting task of introducing a line of foods that most American parents considered superfluous and expensive.

Dan Gerber was convinced that other mothers would enjoy the convenience as much as Dorothy. Before he considered mass-producing the new line, he did some preliminary research among new mothers and learned that convenience was not the chief benefit anticipated from prepared baby food. What mothers most wanted was a wider range of food that included more varieties of fruits and vegetables than they could find year-round at the grocery.

In what was considered a risky and costly advertising campaign in *Good Housekeeping,* six cans of Gerber soup and strained vegetables were offered to the public by mail for $1 and a redeemed coupon that included the name of their favorite grocer. The dollar bills and the coupons poured in. The promotion resulted in national distribution, and by year's end 600,000 cans had been sold.

Dan Gerber had the brilliant idea that an illustration of a cute baby would catch the eye of female readers. To find just the right face, the company sponsored a baby-drawing contest. Artist Dorothy Hope Smith, who submitted a charcoal sketch of a neighbor's child, won. The drawing became famous as the "Gerber Baby," and appeared on the official trademark dated in 1931. For years, a false rumor persisted that the sketch was of Humphrey Bogart as a child, but the star turned out to be Ann Turner, a neighbor's child.

Gerber has faced 73 different competitors in 60 years. Market share for baby food in the United States finds Gerber at **70 percent,** Beech-Nut at 24 percent, and the Earth's Best (Heinz), the first certified organic baby food, at *3½ percent.*

MOTHER KNOWS BEST

Soon Gerber was on the nation's grocery shelves with its original five canned varieties. Within two years, 50 competitors had entered the market. Gerber realized that to maintain its dominance in America, it had to go beyond making nutritious baby food; it had to become more knowledgeable about mothers and babies than any other company. It had to establish itself as *the* baby food company, the one mothers could trust.

LITTLE VITTLES

The first step Gerber took to enhance its reputation was to form relationships with infant nutritionists and pediatricians. The result was an ongoing partnership with the nation's leading baby consultants who helped the company write and prepare baby care publications. Over 50 years ago, these ad hoc professional alliances blossomed into the Gerber Research Center, which is now the largest private industrial complex in the world devoted exclusively to infant nutrition. Dorothy Gerber has contributed by writing a newspaper column called "Bringing Up Baby."

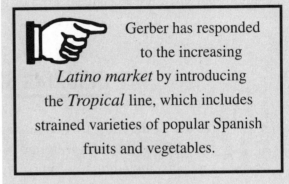

Gerber has responded to the increasing *Latino market* by introducing the *Tropical* line, which includes strained varieties of popular Spanish fruits and vegetables.

BABY BOOMING BUSINESS

The company also has a policy of contacting as many new mothers as they can find, offering nutrition information booklets and cents-off coupons. Lists of new births supplied by pediatricians, nurses, and hospitals have enabled the company to reach 80 percent of all new parents in the United States.

As cans were replaced by jars and the five items grew to more than 250, Gerber Baby Food became a staple of American households of the 1940s. In 1948, Gerber also found the perfect advertising slogan: "Babies are our business, our only business."

LITTLE VITTLES

Gerber later added products for older children. In 1992, the company introduced Gerber Graduates: 23 toddler foods for more mature palates, bakery items, and calcium-enriched juices. The success of this strategy increased the number of jars sold by more than 15 percent annually.

INSURING SUCCESS

With one of the most trusted names in America, it was only a matter of time before the billion-dollar company would introduce other baby products, including toys, nursers, clothing, and safety devices. Gerber even markets life insurance for infants. The "Grow Up" Plan will provide cash (usually, $10,000) when the insured child reaches 21.

Some of the ingredients in Gerber baby food made in other countries include minnows, lamb brains, mung beans, and seaweed.

As the company searches for expanding markets throughout Europe, it hopes to be near $1 billion in sales internationally by the end of the century.

STOCKING STUFFER
L'EGGS

I AM THE EGG MAN

Roger Ferriter was a partner in a design firm whose forte was creating product packaging. In 1968, his company was approached by the Hanes Corporation of Winston-Salem, North Carolina. Hanes needed a package design for a new hosiery line which they intended to sell to mass merchandisers. While contemplating this challenge, Ferriter crumpled a sample pair of the pantyhose in his hand, reducing them to near palm-sized proportions. As he stared at his closed fist, an image appeared: What if the new Hanes hose were sold in an enclosed container instead of a see-through plastic package? What if the product were concealed in "nature's most beautiful package," highlighted with a French twist to the name? Voilà! **L'eggs.**

France's King Henry II wore the **first** fitted hose in **1559.**

A LEG UP

The recent discovery of a post Ice-Age man preserved on a Swiss mountain revealed that he wore leggings made of bark and animal strips. During the Middle Ages, the lower legs of trousers were called breeches, and as these became shorter, fitted legwear called hose covered the lower portion

STOCKING STUFFER

of the leg. In the fourteenth century, close-fitting leggings hugged the skin and displayed every contour of leg, buttocks, and crotch area, which prompted the church to condemn them as immodest. Hose rose to hip level in the fifteenth century. These early "tights" were the forerunners of the one-piece pantyhose.

Stockings date back to 600 A.D. One of the first known references to this apparel is found in a 1306 British manuscript. During Queen Elizabeth's reign, silk stockings became the fashion rage. Later, stockings were held up by garters or suspenders made of fabric or leather. After Reverend William Lee invented the stocking frame in 1589, finely woven stockings were produced by machine.

L'eggs operates more than 100,000 in-store displays nationwide.

Seventeenth century high-fashion hose was made from white silk, and later, white linen or lace. Cotton pervaded in the eighteenth century, increasing in popularity and availability after the Industrial Revolution. But women's stockings would change forever when the E.I. DuPont Company invented nylon in 1938.

WHICH CAME FIRST?

Robert Elberson was hired in 1968 by the Hanes Corporation as president of its hosiery division. Hanes, a textile and clothing manufacturer known for introducing pantyhose, had developed a new material that would stretch but not sag. Sample pantyhose made from the material fit 9 out of 10 women. The one-size-fits-all idea appealed to Elberson who faced a marketing quandary: Go high-end in department stores and specialty shops, or go low-end for volume sales in supermarkets and chain drug stores. He decided on the latter strategy.

STOCKING STUFFER

Elberson first examined the competitive environment. Research indicated that because so many companies manufactured pantyhose, no brand stood out in the consumer's mind. The goal would be to make the Hanes name easily recognizable in stores. That would require major media spending. Enter Ferriter.

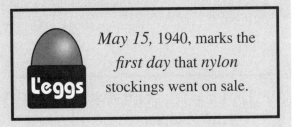

May 15, 1940, marks the *first day* that *nylon* stockings went on sale.

HATCH IT OR NOT?

Once Ferriter had decided on egg-shaped packaging, he and his firm capitalized on the concept by combining the container with the product inside—L'eggs. It was up to Hanes management to gamble millions of dollars on a new product packaged in a kitschy shape and bearing a cute name.

They gave the green light after seeing a free-standing mock display rack that held 24 eggs of pantyhose in various sizes, colors, and styles. The rack also accommodated promotional literature and other information. The consensus was that if retail stores accepted the display, it would stand out from all other pantyhose. Also, by working on consignment, there was no risk for retailers in carrying L'eggs. Hanes would be the owners of the units and rent space from the stores.

WALKING ON L'EGGS

In March 1970, L'eggs was introduced to four test markets. After only six weeks, sales were running at an astounding 1,500 percent above projections. Six months later, Hanes was so confident it released the product nationwide without testing other regional markets. At the end of another six months, 25 percent of all women surveyed in major cities stated that L'eggs

STOCKING STUFFER

was their regular pantyhose brand. First-year sales totaled $9 million; second-year sales climbed to $54 million; and in the third year, the brand generated $112 million.

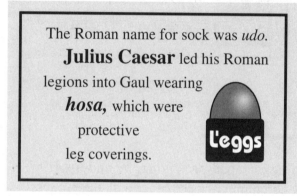

The Roman name for sock was *udo*. **Julius Caesar** led his Roman legions into Gaul wearing *hosa,* which were protective leg coverings.

The advertising campaign was straightforward and memorable, the tag line to the point: "Our L'eggs fit your legs." Before the brand's introduction, the Hanes company had spent only $250,000 annually on advertising. After the launch, expenditures rose to $10 million; and by 1980, Hanes was spending $30 million.

In addition to its successful marketing concepts, L'eggs' major selling feature was that sizing was no longer a guessing game. Women could refer to an easy-to-read chart on the boutique display that pointed to a size that was right for them.

By the beginning of the 1990s, L'eggs commanded a 42 percent market share, with sales totaling over $900 million. Once Hanes became regarded by women as the premiere pantyhose company, it introduced subbrands to meet color, size, style, and seasonal needs. These were the Sheer, Just My Size, and Underalls lines, along with a line of young girls' footwear called Little L'eggs.

The one rotten egg in the venture came when environmentalists began to question the waste caused by millions of plastic egg containers that became non-biodegradable landfill. In 1994, Hanes responded by converting from plastic to environment-friendly cardboard at a 33 percent reduction in cost.

STOCKING STUFFER

Hanes was purchased by the Sara Lee Corporation in 1974. Its new parent paid attention to consumer needs and preferences, and maintained the distribution system which drives profits for both retailer and company. The brand celebrated its 25th anniversary in 1996. It has been worn by millions of American women who delight in opening one of retail's most recognizable packages.

IN THE CHIPS
FRITO-LAY

DEEP IN THE HEART OF TEXAS

n 1932, Elmer Doolin was a small-time ice cream maker in San Antonio, Texas. One day, he stopped off at a cafe for lunch and ordered the 5-cent sandwich special. On an impulse he decided to fork over another nickel for a package of corn chips. The chips were fresher and tastier than he had anticipated, and the single-serve bag seemed just the right size to complement a sandwich. He sought out the man who had made and wrapped the chips, and bought the business for $100. It was well-spent: Doolin owned the man's corn dough recipe, the few retail accounts, and an old hand-operated potato slicer. Doolin started frying the corn chips in his mother's kitchen and selling them to cafes, cantinas, and local grocery stores. He realized he needed a brand name, and to emphasize its south-of-the-border heritage, chose the Spanish word for "fried": **Fritos.**

Frito-Lay employs the **world's largest salesforce** of 12,000, who make 750,000 calls weekly.

IN THE CHIPS

GEORGIA ON MY MIND

In another part of the South, H.W. Lay operated a one-person distribution business in Nashville, Tennessee. He drove his 1929 Model A Ford truck to deliver potato chips made by an Atlanta company. By 1934, Lay had increased sales to include six in-state routes, and was on his way to becoming one of the major Tennessee distributors. Four years later, the Georgia potato chip company experienced financial problems that threatened Lay's supply and livelihood. He borrowed $100, and lined up some other investors to help him buy the potato chip company, changing its name to **Lay's.**

Frito-Lay makes 30,000 snacks per minute.

THIS SPUDS FOR YOU

The snack food industry can trace its ancestry to a native American cook in Saratoga, New York, and a former newspaper salesman from Cleveland, Ohio. In 1853, the railroad magnate Commodore Cornelius Vanderbilt was vacationing at Saratoga Springs, a favorite summer resort of New York's elite families. One night at dinner, he sent the potatoes back to the kitchen complaining that they were "too thick." The cook, George Crum, dutifully sliced a new batch of potatoes, but these were paper-thin, deep fried and salted.

The Commodore loved "crunchy sliced potatoes" and so did his friends. They became a fad among the rich, who demanded those "Saratoga Chips." Soon their popularity extended all over the East Coast where they were available only in fancy restaurants.

IN THE CHIPS

By 1895, the Saratoga Chip was familiar throughout most of America, but not in Cleveland. William Tappenden saw an opportunity to make potato chips a household item. He fried the chips on his kitchen stove and delivered his product from a horse-drawn wagon. In short order, his business increased. Eventually, he converted his barn into the country's first potato chip factory. Soon regional potato chip companies sprouted up all over America.

On the West Coast, in Monterey Park, California, Laura Scudder produced her first chip in 1926. Up to this time, potato chips had been sold in bulk from cracker barrels or from glass cases to the customers. Scudder had the idea to sell her potato chips prepackaged in a bag labeled with her name. The bags were made from sheets of waxed paper by her workers at home.

Vice President Richard *Nixon* took a bag of *corn chips* to Nikita Khrushchev in 1961.

CHIPPING IN

H.W. Lay and Company became one of the largest snack and convenience food companies in the Southeast. Its main product was Lay's Potato Chips, known for their light and crispy crunch. In 1944, H.W. Lay recognized the impact of television and began to advertise locally.

In the meantime, the Fritos Corn Chip Company relocated to Dallas—the hub of Texas commerce—where it experienced rapid growth in sales and distribution. In 1949, it began printing "Fritos brand Golden Chips of Corn" on its bags to bolster its image as the premiere corn chip in the region.

IN THE CHIPS

In 1945, the Frito Company granted the Lay Company exclusive rights to Fritos in the Southeastern region. The result was increased sales for both potato and corn chips.

For the next 16 years, the companies remained separate commercial entities, both prospering in the expanding snack food market. In the 1950s, they began working toward joint national distribution since their salesforces called on the same snack food buyers at the same supermarket chains. Both companies also shared similar philosophies and noncompeting products. A merger finally took place in 1961. Later the same year, the new Frito-Lay Company became a snack food triple threat when it acquired Rold Gold Pretzels.

"BETCHA CAN'T EAT JUST ONE"

Lay started advertising as early as 1944, in Tennessee, with the company's first memorable cartoon character Oscar the Happy Potato. The next step was to sponsor the half-hour children's television cartoon series *Deputy Dawg,* in 1960.

By the early 1960s, snack food sales were skyrocketing, and Lay recognized that it needed to distinguish itself. In one of television's breakthrough campaigns, the company's ad agency produced the famous "Betcha can't eat just one" ad with the incomparable Bert "Cowardly Lion" Lahr as the wide-eyed spokesman.

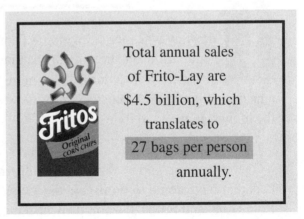

Total annual sales of Frito-Lay are $4.5 billion, which translates to 27 bags per person annually.

IN THE CHIPS

In 1968, comedian Buddy Hackett continued the original campaign with a spin-off tag line: "You can eat a million of 'em, but nobody can eat just one." By 1992, after Lay reformulated the chip to make it crispier and crunchier, ads featured basketball stars Kareem-Abdul Jabbar and Larry Bird, claiming that the chips were "Too good to eat just one."

Frito-Lay dominates the snack food market with **8 out** of the top **10** snacks. The company makes 8.5 billion bags of snacks, and generates $15 billion in sales annually.

Fritos adopted a slew of mascot characters. In 1953, it introduced the Frito Kid, who continued as spokesperson until 1957, followed by the Frito Bandito who turned out to be a public relations problem. Although his name was memorable, the character offended Latino-Americans, and he was dropped. In 1971, the company introduced W.C. Fritos as its new mascot.

THE PEPSI GENERATION

Frito-Lay was merged with the Pepsi-Cola Company in 1965, a brilliant acquisition by the soft drink giant. Today, this snack food division generates worldwide sales of more than $4.5 billion, and accounts for an amazing 40 percent of Pepsico's profits, with operating margins that are among the highest in the food industry.

Over time, the company has successfully introduced different and distinct products that have come to dominate the snack food category. In addition to Lays, Rold Gold, and Fritos, the company also manufactures Ruffles, Doritos, Tostitos, Cheetos, and Sunchips in many flavors and sizes. In response to a new weight-conscious market, more recently, new entries are promoted as low-fat.

IN THE CHIPS

Ed Doolin died in 1959 and H.W. Lay in 1982. Their partnership was steeped in the philosophy to: "Make the best product possible; sell it for a fair profit; and make service a fundamental part of doing business." Their companies had surpassed all expectations, progressing from small but important regional brands into national giants.

BOTTOMS UP
PAMPERS

A CHANGE FOR THE BETTER

 ic Mills was baby-sitting for his first grandchild, and when it was time to change the baby's diaper he found he had a choice: the traditional cloth or an unfamiliar disposable one. Later in the evening when the baby needed a second change, Mills conducted a mini-test of absorbency and convenience. He concluded that cloth had many disadvantages, including laundering and residual odors. On the other hand, the disposable diaper did not provide enough absorbency and lacked sufficient strength.

Mills, an engineer at Proctor & Gamble, told his company about the test, and suggested that there was probably a market for a better product. Procter & Gamble began research that would lead to a radical transformation in the way the world changed its babies: **Pampers.**

> There are more than *15 billion diaper* changes per year in the United States.

BOTTOMS UP

CATCH AS CATCH CAN

he development of diapers coincides with the use of absorbent materials for menstruating women. Paper, wool, vegetable fibers, and grass rolls suited both purposes.

The first cloth used for babies' bottoms was woven of wood and plant matter in the Tigris and Euphrates Valley. One of the most ingenious "diapers" was fashioned by Native American women who stuffed wads of soft moss deep into the bottom of papoose carriers. The concentrated plant substance absorbed liquid and could be replaced on an as-needed basis.

Over the centuries, improvements in the quality of cloth resulted in the diaper with its familiar triangle shape. The diaper pin came into use much later, in the middle of the Industrial Revolution. But cloth and pin improvements aside, the bottom line was that diapers had to be washed, either at home or at the laundry, always an unpleasant and time-consuming task.

During the 1950s, disposable brands—Chux, Dryper and Kleinarts—were available, but they represented less than 1 percent of the nation's diaper changes. Customers found them to be poorly made, often citing problems with wetness control. Moms bought them for traveling purposes only. What was needed was a disposable diaper that didn't leak and was highly absorbent.

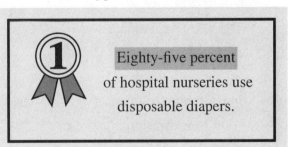

Eighty-five percent of hospital nurseries use disposable diapers.

BOTTOMS UP

P&G R&D

rocter & Gamble has built its reputation on marketing expertise.

Mills's idea for a single-use disposable diaper (this was at the end of the 1950s) would undergo a number of preliminary steps before approval. P&G sought answers to three questions:

1. Did real consumer need exist for an alternative method of diapering?
2. Did P&G have the scientific and technological expertise to develop the product?
3. Did the market have the potential to bring a profit?

In typical P&G fashion, thousands of new mothers were interviewed about diaper usage. Beyond the obvious convenience of a single-use diaper, these moms also raised the issue of rashes caused by the plastic pants worn outside cloth diapers. P&G staff understood that if they could find a solution to the rash problem, they could be the first to satisfy the need.

But one formidable obstacle stood in the way: A machine would have to be designed to make the multi-ply paper diaper. Engineers thought it would be easy to layer three different sheets of material—plastic backing, absorbent padding, and a water-repellent top layer—and then fold them into a zigzag pattern that would be glued together. But the glue applicators dripped. The padding material created mounds of dust. And the glue jammed the equipment. It took 12 months before the machine was running smoothly.

> The best international markets for disposable diapers are *tropical areas*, whose residents don't own washing machines.

BOTTOMS UP

TESTING: ONE, TWO, THREE

y 1961, the kinks had been worked out, and the first disposable diapers were named Pampers, the name believed to best convey tender loving care.

The first test market was Peoria, Illinois, where Pampers were offered for sale at 10 cents per diaper, a price based on the brand generating a profit once it had reached a market volume of 400 million diapers annually. The test proved a disaster; Pampers sold the equivalent of 200 million.

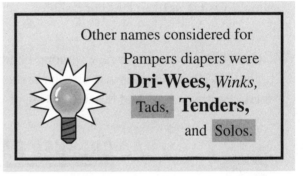

Other names considered for Pampers diapers were **Dri-Wees,** *Winks,* Tads, **Tenders,** and Solos.

Research revealed the price was too high. A second test was conducted in Syracuse, New York, where the diapers were sold for 8 cents each. This proved more successful. Eventually, though, P&G would produce Pampers in volume and lower the price to 6 cents a diaper.

LUV AFFAIRS

ampers' success startled even P&G. In the late 1960s, the disposables represented 25 percent of all diaper changes; essentially, it had the market all to itself. Five years later, half of all babies in the United States wore Pampers. By the late 1970s, the brand controlled 75 percent of all disposable diapers.

BOTTOMS UP

Sensing that competition might challenge its monopoly, P&G came out with Luvs, a premium brand to complement Pampers. Luvs featured extra padding and elastic leg bands to justify its premium price.

Luvs was soon challenged by Kimberly-Clark's Huggies, introduced in the late 1970s. These two high-end diaper brands battled for each and every baby bottom in America, and by 1983, they had carved out a 29 percent share of market—all of which was taken from Pampers' share.

Currently, the price war rages among Pampers, Huggies, and many generic store brands. In 1988, Huggies was on top (or should we say bottom?) with a 30 percent share. Pampers sales had fallen to a low of 28 percent.

GREENER PASTURES

he latest chapter in the disposable diaper story marked the return of the cloth diaper. The growing environmental movement targeted disposable diapers as polluters of the land and decimaters of forests.

In response, the disposable diaper companies have insisted that cloth diapers are just as environmentally unfriendly. They cite the pesticides utilized to grow the cotton, harmful detergents used to wash diapers, and the consumption of energy required to dry the diapers.

The future might bring about the development of ways to recycle disposables, and P&G with its resources and clout will probably be at the forefront of this movement. After all, P&G transformed forever the way the world changed diapers.

EASY LISTENING
BELTONE

SILENT NIGHTS

Sam Posen did not give much thought to the problems of the hearing-impaired. He and his wife Faye lived a comfortable life in Chicago where he worked as a radio technician. But in the late 1930s, the Posens befriended a person with a hearing problem, who complained about his clunky, ineffective, and ugly hearing aid device. Posen wondered why so little progress had been made in this field. An expert in radio technology, it was clear to him that miniature circuitry could accommodate a smaller hearing aid. He wanted the hearing impaired to enjoy the sounds of life "as clear as the tone of a bell": **Beltone.**

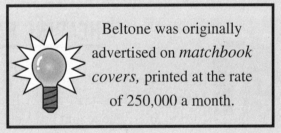

Beltone was originally advertised on *matchbook covers,* printed at the rate of 250,000 a month.

AURAL HISTORY

The earliest method to improve hearing was to cup the hand behind the ear. The Greeks and Romans carved conical hearing aids out of seashells, horns, and antlers.

EASY LISTENING

Trumpet-shaped devices eventually became the standard hearing implements. Two of the early, nonelectrical sound enhancers were the Osteophone and Dentaphone. The Dentaphone user placed a small wooden tongue in the mouth and gripped it tightly between the teeth. Sound was picked up by a silk-covered wire encased in a hand-held diaphragm that carried vibrations first to the teeth then to the bone of the inner ear.

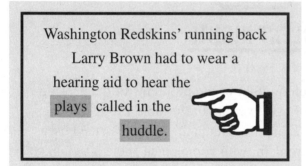

Washington Redskins' running back Larry Brown had to wear a hearing aid to hear the plays called in the huddle.

In the early 1900s, vanity and convenience played important roles in redesigning the shape and size of hearing devices. Smaller instruments were implanted in acoustic beads, ladies' bonnets, opera glasses, fans, and even special chairs to conceal the device.

HEARING REPAIRED

The first electric hearing aid was developed by Miller Hutchinson of Mobile, Alabama, in 1902. It was a large table model that used a carbon microphone and three pairs of earphones. He named the unit the Akoulallion, combining the Greek verbs for "to hear" and "to speak."

The carbon-based unit was improved upon after the vacuum tube was invented by Earl Hanson of the Globe Ear-Phone Company. It provided better amplification without cumbersome microphones. A prototype of this device had been used during World War I to eavesdrop on German troop conversations.

EASY LISTENING

Portable vacuum tube hearing aids signaled a new era for the hearing impaired. Termed "multipacks" or "body boxes," they consisted of two parts: a battery pack (carried in a pocket) attached by wires to the microphone and an amplifier. The body box was not that efficient nor could it be easily concealed.

THE SOUND BARRIER

When the Posens opened the first Beltone office in 1940 in Chicago, they did not know they would revolutionize the field of hearing devices. Nor could they have foreseen that Beltone would be instrumental in launching an organization dedicated to the hearing-impaired, called the Hearing Industries Association.

In that tiny office, Faye Posen tested and fitted customers while Sam built the hearing instruments in the back room. The Posens called their smaller hearing device the Mono-Pac, whose superior benefits required no separate battery pack, no battery wires, and weighed half the amount of other hearing aids.

In short order, other Midwest hearing aid distributors asked to represent the new line, which the Posens had advertised nationally as early as 1944. Faye's brother Dave Barrows became sales manager, and he is credited with organizing an exclusive Beltone distribution network patterned after the insurance business. By 1945, 50 distributorships sold the product.

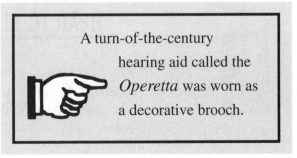

A turn-of-the-century hearing aid called the *Operetta* was worn as a decorative brooch.

EASY LISTENING

The compact Mono-Pac was soon followed by the Harmony (the Posens borrowed from the automobile industry snappy names for their new models). The media praised it as the "ultimate in size reduction." Harmony ads shouted, "Find out why the DEAF call it a miracle." Another ad portrayed a man with his fingers in his ears saying, "Don't shout! My Beltone receiver delivers 2 to 6 times more clear power."

In 1947, the U.S. government permitted printed electronic circuits to be used for nonmilitary purposes. Beltone capitalized on this. By 1948, it had introduced the Symphonette with its "magic silver circuit," marking the first time a printed circuit was used in a civilian product.

In 1808, Johann Malzel invented the first hearing trumpet, the device popularized by his most famous patient Beethoven, for whom he made many models between 1812 and 1814.

The ad campaigns of 1949 emphasized hearing capabilities over miniature size. The print advertisements played upon the fears of men threatened by hearing loss. One read: "DEAFNESS nearly cost me my job! . . . until I discovered this New Invisible Electronic Ear!"

HEAR TO ETERNITY

By 1950, Beltone established a large network of distributorships, and advertised nationally on radio, an odd choice considering the audience they were trying to reach. But with Gabriel Heatter, then a famous radio announcer, as spokesperson, new sales leads poured in.

EASY LISTENING

The introduction of the Melody model that year was accompanied by a memorable public relations promotion. With the background theme "A Melody is Like a Pretty Girl," two female models clad in see-through cellophane dresses displayed the hearing aid on their bras.

The first National Hearing Aid Society Convention was held in 1951, and three years later, Dave Barrows was elected president. He helped draft the first Code of Ethics as part of the movement to legitimize the Society the way opticians and optometrists had theirs.

The first Hear-N-See combination eyeglass and hearing aid was introduced by Beltone in 1956. But the big news came in 1958 when the Minuet, the first behind-the-ear aid, was introduced. It offered the hearing-impaired an almost invisible device located where it would do the most good—flush with the ear.

The Posen's son Larry, a Purdue engineering graduate, is credited with inventing the Beltone Micro-Module circuit. He became president of the company in 1974. Beltone hired actor Eddie Albert in 1988 as spokesman for the company's line of improved miniature hearing aids sold under the Alto-Max brand name.

Sam Posen died in 1981. Over his lifetime, he had seen the rise of an entire industry: The FDA had approved regulations granting hearing aid specialists a new stature; Congress had created a network of health care professionals through the new National Institute for Communication Disorders. A man who had acted on a friend's complaint ultimately brought the sounds of life to the hearing-impaired.

PADS OF GLORY

S.O.S

ALUMINUM SITINGS

dwin Cox went door to door, selling Wear-Ever aluminum cookware. The year was 1917 and the city was San Francisco. One day turned out to be especially slow, and he pondered whether the strenuous climb up and down the steep hills of the city was worth it. Although he was convinced that aluminum offered an inexpensive and more efficient way to prepare meals than copper or iron, he couldn't figure out why the aluminum cooking line met with consumer resistance. The answer came from a former customer who vowed she would never buy aluminum again because it was too hard to keep clean.

Cox put two and two together: If he could solve the cleaning problem, his cookware sales would increase. He experimented at home, and hit upon a combination of thin steel wool packed with soap. He made the steel wool balls in his basement by dipping them into a hand-grade liquid soap and then hanging the spheres

> S.O.S soap pads start as a coil of steel *17 miles long.*

on a clothesline to dry. His wife suggested a name for this new kitchen helper: She called it "Save Our Saucepans"—when abbreviated, it became **S.O.S**.

PADS OF GLORY

CLEANING UP

The Industrial Revolution produced the ironware that eventually found its way into every kitchen in western Europe and the United States. Initially, a mixture of sand and lye soap was used to clean these heavy iron skillets, pots, and pans. The solvent was applied with wire or iron brushes. A different mixture of ashes and soap was used to remove fatty or oily residue.

SCOURING THE NATION

Cox carried the pads with him on his door-to-door rounds. To his surprise, customers were more interested in the wool-soap concoction than the pots and pans. Housewives liked the convenience, and the little soap pad scoured as promised. Cox patented the invention and the S.O.S name in 1918.

Capital was raised by selling patent rights on a geographical basis in 11 western states in 1919. Subsequently, small plants were built in San Francisco and later in Chicago. For the next 16 years, S.O.S had the scouring pad business locked up. During this period, American householders found other nonkitchen uses for the handy soap pad. It cleaned aluminum screens, whitewall tires, metal sports equipment, tools, and

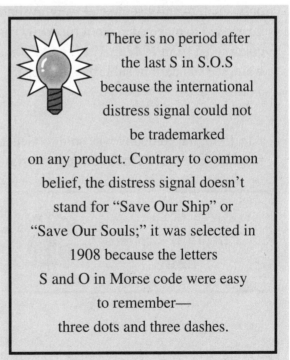

There is no period after the last S in S.O.S because the international distress signal could not be trademarked on any product. Contrary to common belief, the distress signal doesn't stand for "Save Our Ship" or "Save Our Souls;" it was selected in 1908 because the letters S and O in Morse code were easy to remember— three dots and three dashes.

PADS OF GLORY

more. Because the wool was of such a fine grade of steel, S.O.S pads did not scratch surfaces, and restored grimy tools to pristine condition.

SHAPING UP AND SHIPPING OUT

The S.O.S patent expired after 17 years in 1935, and waiting in the wings were other companies ready to cash in on the soap pad market. Faced with competition for the first time, S.O.S introduced the oval-shaped pad familiar to users today. S.O.S invested more in advertising to meet the challenge from the new competitors.

When United States entered World War II, steel production was rationed, and only small quantities of steel were available for household use. S.O.S was commissioned to make steel wool for Army camouflage. After the war, soap pad sales quadrupled from 1947 to 1957, paralleling the increased sale of aluminum cookware, the standard in suburban kitchens.

In 1958, the company was sold to General Foods, which altered the soap color from pink to blue. This seemingly insignificant change later became the main component of a historic advertising campaign that would help to establish S.O.S as the nation's number-one soap pad.

America uses
2 million soap pads
daily.

PADS OF GLORY

SOAP PAD WARS

Miles Laboratories purchased S.O.S from General Foods for $55 million in 1968. Miles Labs was well known as the maker of Alka-Seltzer, whose television commercials in the late 1960s were created by Doyle Dane Bernbach ("I can't believe I ate the whole thing" and "Speecy Spicy Meatball"). These ads brought humor into the hum-drum analgesic category. Miles turned to DDB to promote its soap pad product.

Over the years, Brillo had become the dominant soap pad brand in the New York market. DDB's creative team pursued a one-on-one competitive strategy, demonstrating that S.O.S pads contained more soap and lasted longer. The ensuing campaign pitted "Big Blue" against "Pink Pad." Brillo was never mentioned by name. In the first campaign, an animated water pistol shootout portrayed blue S.O.S emerging the winner against the pink pad.

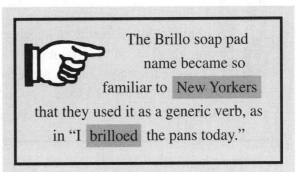

The Brillo soap pad name became so familiar to New Yorkers that they used it as a generic verb, as in "I brilloed the pans today."

In 1994, the Clorox Company purchased S.O.S from Miles Labs. With Clorox as its new owner—the fourth in the company's history—the product is still sold in the familiar yellow box with blue soap pads.

THE YELLOW PAGES
POST-IT NOTES

TURNING SILVER INTO GOLD

 rthur Fry loved to sing in his church choir. What he didn't love was losing his place in the hymn book even after he inserted scraps of paper between the pages. On many occasions, the little paper markers fluttered out. Fry, a scientist at the 3M Company in St. Paul, Minnesota, recalled an "unglue" adhesive that had been developed years earlier by a coworker named Dr.

The original name of Post-it Notes was **Press and Peel.**

Spencer Silver. Silver's adhesive had one unusual property: it was strong enough to grip, yet could be easily removed. Fry would eventually develop a more practical and widespread use for the "un-glue": **Post-it Notes.**

HOLD FAST

 ver since the spoken word became the written, scribes have sought ways to attach pages. The Romans solved the problem by rolling parchment sheets into long tubes. In medieval times, paper sheets were tied with ribbon or string inserted through tiny knife slits in the upper left-hand corner of the pages.

THE YELLOW PAGES

Some early wire fasteners resembled the snap-spring devices found on clip-boards. But serrated edges poked jagged holes in the paper they held together. A simpler metallic fastener was needed.

A Norwegian named Johan Vaaler is credited with the invention of the paper clip in 1899. A Yank named Cornelius Brosnan designed a paper clip featuring rounded edges and an inner loop. He called it the Konaclip, and it was made with "eyes" inside a wire frame to reduce snaring other clips.

> The light yellow color was chosen for Post-its because it contrasted with white office correspondence.

Financial success would, however, belong to the Gem Company which, in 1899, secured a patent not for a paper clip but for a machine to mass-produce them. By 1908, Gem could proudly advertise itself as America's "most popular clip."

FRY IT UP

Fry arrived at work eager to investigate the bookmark potential of "un-glue." 3M had initiated a policy called bootlegging, which permitted its scientists to spend up to 15 percent of their time on pet projects. Initially, the adhesive was too strong. Fry said, "Some of the hymnal pages I tested my first notes on are probably still stuck together."

The next stage, making notepaper slips, took only 18 months. 3M's marketing department was unimpressed: Why would consumers pay a premium price for adhesive notepaper when they could use scrap paper for free?

A second obstacle came from 3M's mechanical engineers who doubted that an adhesive could ever be uniformly applied to a section of paper. Undaunted, Fry assembled a machine in his basement that successfully overcame the adhesive application.

THE PAPER TRAIL

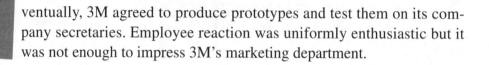

Eventually, 3M agreed to produce prototypes and test them on its company secretaries. Employee reaction was uniformly enthusiastic but it was not enough to impress 3M's marketing department.

3M test marketed in four cities, where sales were acceptable but not outstanding. But when executives looked more closely at the data, they noticed that some dealers had experienced off-the-chart sales. The company questioned these dealers and discovered one constant—free samples.

3M took the idea and conducted a final test, kicked off by massive free sampling. The company hired temps from the Manpower agency to provide live demonstrations. A 50-percent "purchase intent" would have been considered excellent; Post-its scored a phenomenal 90 percent.

By 1980, the product hit the entire United States, and in 1981, it was introduced to Europe. In 1983, sales totaled $45 million, and for a number of years increased at a reputed growth rate of 85 percent. By 1984, Post-its became the most successful new product in 3M's history.

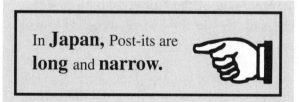

In **Japan,** Post-its are **long** and **narrow.**

THE YELLOW PAGES

A FINAL NOTE

3M sought to expand sales by developing new concepts and sizes for the notes. The initial sizes were 1½ × 2 inches and 3 × 5 inches, to which a 5 × 8-inch size was added. In 1981, the company introduced a Post-it Note Tray so that sloppy users could keep the handy notes in one place. In 1985, the brand expanded to include multi- and neon-colored pads. Distributorships began to sell them with preprinted messages, company names, and logos.

Today, Post-its rank among the top four office supply products, along with copier paper, file folders, and cellophane tape. Its success belongs to Arthur Fry, who was given the company's Carlton Society Award, its most prestigious scientific achievement. A genial choir singer had taken a colleague's technology and turned it into a multimillion dollar item.

The most unusual consumer promotion for Post-its came from a family that stuck a *"Baby sleeping"* message on their front door. It hung there through the gale force winds of *Hurricane Hugo.*

LITTLE DIPPER

DIXIE CUPS

PAPER WORKS

On a hot August day in 1909, Old Zeke drove into his dusty Kansas hometown to buy grain feed. He paused for a refreshing drink from the well located in the middle of Main Street that had provided water for horses and townspeople since 1804. Zeke took a couple of man-sized swigs from the community dipper. A month later, Old Zeke died a horrible death caused by hepatitis.

Zeke is just a figment of the imagination, a symbol of the many who died in similar fashion. The State of Kansas's Commissioner of Health, Samuel Crumbine, MD, was certain victims contracted diseases from germs transferred through public water sources. States soon passed legislation to outlaw public drinking vessels, which were rarely washed or sterilized. It would be a Harvard dropout from Kansas named Hugh Moore who would replace these public ladles with **Dixie Cups.**

> "Dixie Cups" was the product's fourth name; a previous name was Health Kups.

LITTLE DIPPER

TROUBLED WATERS

Water. Life can't exist without it. But contaminated water can kill. Epidemics of cholera or dysentery resulted from water fouled by human waste. When Robert Koch, the nineteenth-century German scientist, proved that unseen bacteria caused infectious diseases, it became apparent that many of these microorganisms lived in water. It would be many years before the world's population recognized that the communal dipper carried these deadly germs.

In the first decade of the twentieth century, American scientists investigated the transference of germs in public places. Professor Alvin Davison of Lafayette College in Pennsylvania examined public drinking cups under a microscope and found communicable germs. Thanks to the Crumbine/Kansas laws and Davison's research, one by one, state legislatures passed laws prohibiting communal drinking vessels in the town or the factory.

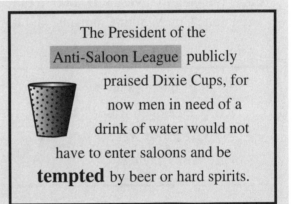

The President of the Anti-Saloon League publicly praised Dixie Cups, for now men in need of a drink of water would not have to enter saloons and be **tempted** by beer or hard spirits.

PUBLIC ASSISTANCE

Hugh Moore's original idea was to make cool water available publicly. In 1908, he invented a handy dispenser from which a cool drink could be had for a penny. The dispenser was a white porcelain decanter divided into three sections: the upper part held a cake of ice, the middle contained a five-gallon bottle of spring water, and the bottom held a drain for waste water. For a

LITTLE DIPPER

penny, customers received 5 ounces in a cup with a flat bottom and a rough lip. A receptacle for discarded cups was placed next to the dispenser. Moore also distributed literature to explain that cups could be thrown away or kept, but never reused.

HIS CUP DIDN'T RUNNETH OVER

or a while Moore broke even financially with his water machines, but his ultimate goal was to design a cup dispenser, not a water dispenser. He searched for capital and finally convinced the president of the American Can Company to invest $200,000 in the venture. The new company was named The Public Cup Vendor Company, and it incorporated in 1909.

The most memorable Dixie Cup slogan was *"Quaff Nature's Nectar from this chalice."*

The next year, the company was renamed the Individual Drinking Cup Company. Moore hoped that the public dipper's bad reputation would make his sanitary cups an easy sale. But, people were not convinced.

The nation's railroads also resisted (Dr. Crumbine's Kansas legislation stipulated that shared drinking cups were prohibited on passenger trains running through the state). Finally, though, railroad companies ordered the cups, including the Lackawanna Railroad which carried many female passengers. Moore penned an advertising ditty especially for these women:

"Phoebe dear, you need not fear,

To drink from cups that you find here.

With cups of white, no bugs will bite.

Upon the road of anthracite."

LITTLE DIPPER

In 1912, Moore changed the name of his company a third time to Health Kups. He thought soda fountains might provide a prime market. The drawback was door-to-door sales. Even when a soda shop owner was interested, profit and loss proved faulty. A dishwasher's weekly salary was less than the purchase of 1,000 cups. And glassware was reusable.

WHISTLING DIXIE

By 1919, Hugh Moore was a 10-year veteran of the cup business. He was unsatisfied with his progress. Perhaps the name Health Cups conveyed an antiseptic and medicinal image. He began to search for a name with more pizzazz.

One day, Moore visited a company in his building called the Dixie Doll Company. Its owner did not know the origins of the name Dixie, so Moore recounted the tale told to him as a boy by his grandfather. According to legend, in the 1820s, state banks could issue their own money. One of the most famous was a bank in New Orleans that had earned a reputation among the riverboat men on the Mississippi for the reliability of its currency. The most common legal tender the New Orleans bank printed was a $10 bill with the word *dix* (ten in French) written across each note. The riverboat men called these bills "dixies," mispronouncing the French X. This area of New Orleans became known as "Dixie Land."

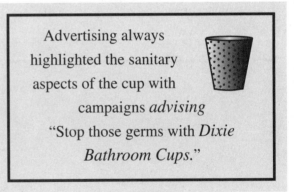

Advertising always highlighted the sanitary aspects of the cup with campaigns *advising* "Stop those germs with *Dixie Bathroom Cups*."

In recounting the story, the word Dixie struck a chord. It was short. It was easy to remember. Its history was quaint. And with the word Cup, it created a nice rhythm: Dixie Cup.

LITTLE DIPPER

SUNDAE TIMES

oore's big break came from the ice cream industry. Traditionally, ice cream was sold in half-pint, pint, and gallon containers or in glass servers at fountains. The ice cream companies sought to compete with individually wrapped candy bars and bottled soft drinks for the single, take-away purchase. But they needed a vessel for single servings of ice cream. The answer was the Dixie Cup.

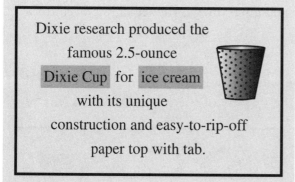

Dixie research produced the famous 2.5-ounce Dixie Cup for ice cream with its unique construction and easy-to-rip-off paper top with tab.

Today, we take for granted water coolers with paper-cup dispensers. We drink and discard the paper cup, and no one worries about germs or disease thanks to Hugh Moore's handy little dispenser.

HOUSE OF WAX
CRAYOLA

PIGMENT OF THEIR IMAGINATION

Joseph W. Binney founded the Peekskill (New York) Chemical Company in 1864 to sell color-based products, such as the charcoal and red iron oxide-based paints used to coat barns. In 1885 it expanded the product line to include shoe polish, slate pencils, and a chalk called An-Du-Septic-Dustless, which schoolteachers loved. It was the schoolteachers who implored the company to manufacture an inexpensive crayon.

After years of research, in 1903, the company produced its first box of crayons. Binney's daughter-in-law was asked to name the newly designed green and yellow box. She combined the French word for chalk or stick of color, *craie,* and added the suffix *ola,* shortened from oleaginous (oily). Americans would know Binney & Smith's "oily chalk color stick" by its beloved name: **Crayola.**

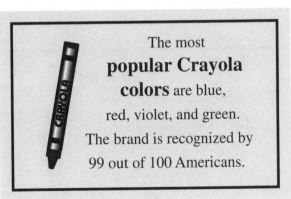

The most **popular Crayola colors** are blue, red, violet, and green. The brand is recognized by 99 out of 100 Americans.

COLORFUL MOMENTS

Crayons were first used in the eighteenth century in Europe. Early prototypes were made from a mixture of charcoal and oil poured in cylinders that resembled hollow sticks. Later in that century, various pigments were added, and wax replaced charcoal and oil.

During the nineteenth century in the United States, if schools wanted to supply crayons for children, they had to import them from Europe. This proved too costly for the many one-room schoolhouses that dotted the American landscape.

Binney & Smith's researchers first developed a one-color (carbon black) crayon stick made of wax to mark crates and barrels. The next step in the development was to find nontoxic pigments, because young children liked to chew on the crayons.

The company's first green and yellow crayon box described the contents as "School Crayons for Educational Color Work." The original eight colors were black, blue, brown, green, orange, red, violet, and yellow.

In 1996, the 100 billionth Crayola rolled off the assembly line. It was periwinkle blue, and the guest of honor for the event was television's Mister Rogers.

Crayola helped one American child on the prairie win first prize in a local drawing contest. The artist was Grant Wood, the painter of "American Gothic," who remembered fondly that Crayola gave him his start.

HOUSE OF WAX

SHAPING UP

In 1885, Binney & Smith used its storehouse of chemical research to perfect crayons. Today the company still follows a century-old method. First, paraffin is liquified, then it is poured into a mold containing 2,400 slots. The wax is cooled by water. Each color requires a specific cooling period, varying from four to seven minutes.

After cooling, the crayons are hydraulically ejected from the molds. Crayons with broken tips, chipped ends, or uneven colors are returned to the mixing vat to be remelted and remodeled. Finally, the

Over time, **political correctness** dictated name changes for some crayon colors. To wit: Prussian Blue became Midnight Blue. Flesh was changed to Peach to reflect diversity of skin color.

crayons are inserted into a machine that attaches the labels. Although crayons today are made in 112 different colors, labels come in only 18 shades. For extra strength, each label is wrapped around the crayon twice.

The Crayola crayon follows industry standards set by the Art & Craft Material Institute to minimize customer confusion.

ART TOTS

Crayola crayons are safe, long-lasting, and provide hours of rainy-day activity. Today, the average American child spends 30 minutes a day coloring. That constitutes 6.3 billion hours of coloring annually.

HOUSE OF WAX

For art students, Binney & Smith added the Rubens crayon line in the 1920s.

> Crayons rank **18** among the top **20** recognizable American **scents.**
> Coffee and peanut butter are 1 and 2.

In 1936, the company became a founding member of the Crayon, Watercolor, and Craft Institute, which promotes product safety in art materials. In 1948, the company instituted a teacher workshop program to offer guidelines for educating schoolchildren about art and color.

COLOR CORNUCOPIA

When, in 1949, Binney & Smith decided to add new colors to the basic eight, America waited to see the new choices. By 1957, there were 48 colors, and later 24 more were added. Many hues duplicated oil paint colors—raw sienna, burnt orange, and plum. To keep up with modern design, Binney & Smith added "hot" colors: atomic tangerine, screaming green, and shocking pink.

In 1990, the company retired eight colors—raw umber, maize, lemon yellow, blue gray, violet blue, orange yellow, green blue, and orange red—to "The Crayola Hall of Fame." So popular were these colors that protest groups petitioned for their reinstatement. The groups even created acronyms for the doomed colors, including RUMPS (Raw Umber and Maize Preservation Society) and CRAYON (Committee to Reestablish All Your Old Norms).

Binney & Smith introduced eight new hues the same year. They were bold and bright and consistent with colors kids wanted: cerulean, fuchsia, vivid tangerine, and wild strawberry.

HOUSE OF WAX

In 1992, Binney & Smith came out with its "Global Pack," eight multicultural colors that reflected a full range of human skin tones. In 1993, 16 more crayons were born, for a grand total of 96 colors. In a public relations coup, Binney & Smith invited consumers to name these newest entries. Two million people sent in suggestions. Don't blame the company if you don't like timberwolf, wisteria, macaroni and cheese, or tropical rain forest. And if you do, you'll have to contact Hallmark which purchased Binney & Smith in 1984.

THE CANDY MAN

TOOTSIE ROLL

ON A ROLL

 eo Hirshfield was a wide-eyed and ambitious Austrian immigrant who arrived in America in 1896 looking for the good life. His family settled into a New York City rooming house and he walked the streets to sample the local candy. He ate toffee and taffy, nut clusters and horehound mints, peppermints and caramels. Hirshfield was delighted at what he didn't find: a chocolately, chewy candy. Inside his pocket was a recipe for just such a tasty sweet. Hirschfield seized the opportunity. His wife suggested he name the confection after their daughter Clara. He agreed, but instead used 5-year-old Clara's nickname, Tootsie: **Tootsie Roll.**

The Sweets Company of America was the Tootsie Roll company's original name. In 1922, sales were $1.3 million; in 1996, they reached $313 million.

SWEET SENSATIONS

 n 1893, Milton Hershey started producing the Chocolate Almond and Milk Chocolate Bars that the world knows and enjoys today. At that time, the Hershey Company also manufactured McGinties Caramels—which were bean-shaped and sold 10 for a penny—Jim Cracks, Uniques, Empires, and Coconut Irises.

THE CANDY MAN

To the greenhorn Hirshfield in 1896, Hershey must have seemed like daunting competition. But the Austrian was counting on two distinct differences: his candy's unique shape (the roll was a stark contrast to the rectangular bars) and the promise of a long-lasting chew.

The first batch of Tootsie Rolls was produced in Brooklyn, New York. The early years were taxing, but Hirshfield managed to secure a foothold in New York City and neighboring eastern markets. The whimsical name helped consumers to remember the bite-size candy, the first American sweet to be sold as a paper-wrapped single.

By 1904, as demand increased, Hirshfield incorporated his fledgling company. A year later, he moved Tootsie Roll production to a four-story candy factory in Manhattan. Everyone in America was falling in love with the tasty chocolately-chewy roll.

In 1917, the Roll was on a roll. When America's Expeditionary Force sailed to France, the candy was a standard component of every doughboy's rations. The tiny confection stayed fresh in its wrapper, tasted delicious, and provided a sugary burst of quick energy. A Tootsie Roll poster at war's end showed crowds welcoming Yanks with the statement: "When the Boys Come Home. The Greatest Deserve the Best. Tootsie Roll." That same year the company's name was changed to Sweets Company of America. And five years later, in 1922, it registered with the New York Stock Exchange.

LIFE SAVER

he Tootsie Pop was introduced in 1931, featuring a fruit-flavored hard candy shell surrounding the familiar soft chocolately-chewy Tootsie Roll. It was an immediate hit with American kids.

THE CANDY MAN

In 1938, when the New York City location proved too small for the burgeoning company, it moved across the Hudson River to Hoboken, New Jersey. The new 35,000-square-foot facility featured a conveyer belt system to mass-produce the two products.

Tootsie Roll accompanied GIs into battle when America entered World War II. The candy was highly prized for its ability to withstand all weather conditions, from freezing cold in Alaska's Aleutian Island bases to the tropical heat of the North African campaign. Along the victory trail from Normandy to Berlin, the little American treat won friends as soldiers tossed handfuls to the liberated throngs.

World War II fighter pilot Frederick Arnold wrote in his autobiography *Doorknob Five Two* of how Tootsie Rolls saved his life. When his plane was shot down and he parachuted into the Sahara Desert, he had nothing to eat but Tootsie Rolls. After trekking through the desert for a number of hours, he rewarded himself with one segment of the candy. He survived for three days before he encountered a North African tribe who welcomed him—only after he handed out Tootsie Rolls.

Sammy Davis threw Tootsie Rolls to the audience when he was starring in the Broadway show *Candy Man.*

DAVID AMONG THE GOLIATHS

In 1948, under the aegis of the company's new president William Rubin, Tootsie Roll sponsored children's television shows including *Howdy Doody, Rin Tin Tin,* and *Rocky and Bullwinkle.* In a print ad, run in a 1950 issue of *Life* magazine, the smiling young woman posing with a Tootsie Roll was Rubin's daughter Ellen. Today, Ellen Gordon is the president of the company.

THE CANDY MAN

The Rubin family continues to demonstrate that a unique candy can compete with chocolate giants Hershey and Nestlé. Though the company achieves only a small 2 percent-plus market share of the over $10 billion candy category, Tootsie Roll continues to be number one among taffies and lollipops.

The company is often cited as one of the best managed in the country, and has made *Forbes'* honor roll of small companies. One reason for its continued success is the family's hands-on control: from raw materials, recipe, packaging, and advertising—which is done in-house by its own ad agency. Future plans are to import to Europe and the Far East, areas that have confectionery consumption 40 percent higher per capita than in the United States.

International expansion of the Tootsie Roll company began in *Mexico* where the candy is known as *"Tutsi."*

In his novel *Triple,* Ken Follett wrote: "Girls will do anything for a Tootsie Roll." And in Ross Thomas's novel *The Eighth Dwarf,* one character asks rhetorically, "Can you imagine a conquering nation with a sweet called Tootsie Rolls?"

A STITCH IN TIME
SINGER SEWING MACHINE

STREET SINGER

Isaac Merritt Singer was born in Pittstown, New York, in 1811. At age 12, he ran away to join a troupe of traveling street performers. He was also a machinist, who had invented a wood block for the manufacturing of printing type. While visiting Boston in 1850, he stopped at a machine shop where Orson Phelps had attempted to manufacture a new sewing machine. Singer studied Phelp's model and made three design suggestions, then implemented the improvements himself, thereby creating the Perpendicular Action Belay Stitch Machine, which he patented in 1851. Later, Singer took the machine to fairs and church socials to demonstrate the ease and speed of machine stitching versus time-consuming handwork.

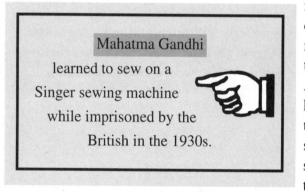

Mahatma Gandhi learned to sew on a Singer sewing machine while imprisoned by the British in the 1930s.

Orders came from garment manufacturers, and soon word reached Elias Howe, who had secured the first sewing machine patent in 1846. In 1854, Howe knocked on Singer's door and demanded $25,000 for patent infringement. Ultimately, a smart New York lawyer made everyone rich and brought machine sewing into millions of homes worldwide via **Singer Sewing Machines.**

A STITCH IN TIME

AND HOWE

The Massachusetts-born Elias Howe invented the lock-stitching sewing machine, a device that could sew 250 stitches per minute. His first model failed because the machine could not accurately emulate the action of a human arm. In the second model, he perfected the machine and added a needle and an intermittent thread feed. But it was Singer's innovative foot treadle and yielding presser foot that made the machine truly practical.

Singer knew that Howe's lawsuit could spell financial ruin, so he sought out a young lawyer from New York City named Edward Clark. Clark took on the case in exchange for one-third ownership in the Singer Company's flourishing business. The lawyer realized that if all parties cooperated, everyone would benefit from Howe's patent and Singer's ingenuity.

In 1854, Clark succeeded in bringing together 24 American sewing companies in the nation's first patent pool called the Sewing Machine Combination. Under the provisions of the arrangement, sewing machines would sell for $15, and Singer and Howe each would receive $5 for every one sold domestically. The agreement lasted until 1877 when the patent expired.

Howe smartly agreed to the consortium settlement, because by that time, Singer's company had captured the lion's share of the market, and he was without a factory to manufacture his machines.

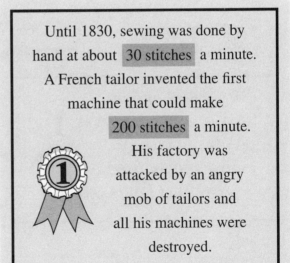

Until 1830, sewing was done by hand at about 30 stitches a minute. A French tailor invented the first machine that could make 200 stitches a minute. His factory was attacked by an angry mob of tailors and all his machines were destroyed.

A STITCH IN TIME

Eventually, Howe opened a plant in Bridgeport, Connecticut. He grew rich from the millions of dollars earned from Combination royalties. He even supported an entire infantry regiment, in which he served as a private, during the Civil War.

ALL SEWN UP

Although Singer proved to be the inventive and mechanical mind behind the works, it was Clark's business foresight that brought the sewing machine and the Singer name to the forefront of the world market. He was the first to recognize that sewing machines could be sold beyond the tailor and garment manufacturing industries, into the untapped market of seamstresses and housewives.

Clark promised to pay $50 to anyone who brought in a used machine of any manufacturer as a down payment on the purchase of a new Singer model. This first-of-its-kind promotion tripled Singer's sales by 1856.

Clark's second brainstorm was a concept called installment selling, which enabled an average American homemaker to afford the $125 machine. He introduced the "Hire-Purchase Plan" with terms of $5 down and $3 per month. To promote this strategy, the gimmick-minded Clark also offered prominent and respected women a 50-percent discount.

> The Singer Company billed its sewing machines as "the best-known and **most widely used product** in the world."

A STITCH IN TIME

Clark also hired and trained professional seamstresses to demonstrate in the front windows of retail stores the ease of working with the machines. Passersby would stop and marvel at the creations being stitched by means of a simple press and release of the foot pedal.

In 1863, the partnership between Clark and Singer dissolved, reportedly because Singer's untoward personal life became public knowledge. He was said to have fathered 24 children from four women. When public outcry threatened to escalate, he escaped to England where he continued his extravagant lifestyle until he died in 1875. Clark stayed on as president of the company until his death in 1882.

GIANT'S STEPS

Eight years after Singer started selling machines in 1853, the company sold models in Europe and, by 1867, manufactured in England. Gradually, factories opened all over Europe. In 1910, the company's Scottish branch at Clydebank was the world's largest, encompassing some 450,000 square feet and employing more than 3,500 workers. It was the only railway station in Great Britain named after a factory.

Because the Singer machines could be built from local steel and wood, the manufacturing process was easily adapted to foreign locales. In Imperial Russia, one of the Czar's major attempts to start the Industrial Revolution in his country was to build a Singer manufacturing facility outside of Moscow. The vast Russian market made it the number-one country for Singer sales in the world.

ORIENT EXPRESS

Sales of sewing machines in the United States declined by 50 percent from the beginning of the 1970s to the middle of the 1980s. It was cheaper to buy ready-to-wear clothing than to sew. At the same time, the

A STITCH IN TIME

Singer company was hard-pressed to compete with the emerging competition from Japan, Taiwan, and South Korea.

In 1992, Singer Sewing Machine was acquired by International-SemiTech Microelectronics, a multinational conglomerate based in Hong Kong. It entered into a $20 million joint venture with the Shanghai Sewing Machine Company to sell moderately priced machines to the vast Chinese market.

The name Singer still evokes an image of quality, efficiency, and style. It is one of 25 products that has retained a number-one position in market share since this statistic was first measured in 1923. Mahatma Gandhi said it best: "The sewing machine was one of the few useful things ever invented."

HOME COOKING
BOSTON MARKET

BOY WONDERS

They saturate the landscape of the United States: fast-food franchises selling hamburgers, pizza, sandwiches, fried chicken, roast beef, Mexican food, cookies, yogurt, doughnuts, ice cream, and more. It seemed unlikely that there was room for another. But in 1985, Arthur Cores, a 33-year-old manager of a gourmet grocery store, and his friend Steven Kolow, a 29-year-old real estate manager, reasoned that people who had no time to cook would enjoy take-out, "home-cooked" meals. Cores and Kolow borrowed recipes from their grandmothers for chicken soup, oatmeal cookies, and other standards. The menu was simple: marinated chicken roasted in a brick-fired rotisserie, "real" mashed potatoes, fresh squash, and cornbread. With a $40,000 investment, they opened a store in Newton, Massachusetts, in December 1985 and kept the name simple, too: **Boston Chicken.**

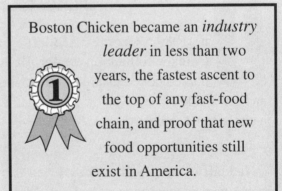

Boston Chicken became an *industry leader* in less than two years, the fastest ascent to the top of any fast-food chain, and proof that new food opportunities still exist in America.

HOME COOKING

FRANCHISE FEVER

In the national business boom of the 1950s, resurrection of an old business strategy called franchising offered thousands of Americans the opportunity to go into business for themselves. The concept was simple: A well-known, nationally advertised retail business would "sell" the rights to duplicate its operation in exchange for a start-up fee and a royalty percentage on all future sales. In addition, the parent company would train the new owner to operate the business to the exact standards of the chain. Each week a percentage of the gross sales, plus an additional amount for advertising and marketing, would be returned to the head office.

> Originally, Boston Chicken offered franchises only to those with proven track records running other fast-food chains.

AMERICA ON LINE

In 1989, George Naddaff was sent by his wife to Boston Chicken to pick up dinner. He looked at the menu; it offered a basic home-cooked meal—roast chicken dinner with mashed potatoes, salad, and other side dishes. And the restaurant was filled with the wonderful aromas of a kitchen at Thanksgiving.

Naddaff owned 19 Kentucky Fried Chicken stores and recognized that this home-cooked meal concept had franchise potential. He also headed a venture capital company that found resources for start-up companies. He returned frequently to the location to chat with customers and finally talked to the owners too.

HOME COOKING

Cores and Kolow had turned down other buyers for fear of losing control of the business. But Naddaff presented himself as someone who knew the food business and did not want to change their basic concept. Under the terms of the deal, Cores and Kolow sold the rights to Boston Chicken but retained ownership of the original store. They also received stock in the newly formed company. Kolow stayed on to manage the restaurant while Cores joined the new entity, New Boston Chicken, Inc., as head of product development.

Naddaff opened two new stores, which proved as successful as the original location. The stores' hot take-out meals, retailing for about $6, had widespread appeal. By 1990, there were 13 stores in New England, generating $8 million in sales; and by 1991, there were 29 and more than $21 million in sales.

Boston Chicken was voted **America's** *favorite* **chicken** *chain* by *Restaurants and Institutions* magazine.

A CHICKEN IN EVERY POT

Saad Nadhir, a partner in Blockbuster Entertainment, spotted a long line of people waiting outside a Boston Chicken outlet in Newton, Massachusetts. He entered, looked at the operation, and later returned with colleague Scott Beck.

Beck was a business wunderkind. Years earlier, he had talked his father into buying some of the first Blockbuster franchises and convinced Wayne Huzienga to purchase the company and take it public. At age 33, Beck had sold his share of Blockbuster Video for $120 million. He was anxious to find another million-dollar franchise venture, and he saw that potential in Boston Chicken.

HOME COOKING

In May 1992, a newly formed partnership with Nadhir, Beck, and a third investor acquired a controlling interest in Boston Chicken, Inc. In the purchase, Cores, Kolow, and Naddaff became wealthy overnight.

> Symbolically, the 1,000th Boston Chicken store opened in Boston in 1996.

By December 1993, the new owner-management team moved its headquarters to Chicago and in that year opened 182 new restaurants. They sold shares on NASDAQ, with an initial public offering that raised $54 million. In August 1994, nine months after the NASDAQ listing, the stock split two for one. Investors were interested in the company's claims that by year-end it would open its 500th store. In La Brea, California, 3,000 miles from Boston, it did.

FAST TRACK TO MARKET

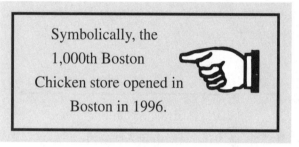

The new owners and their team of experienced fast-food industry executives decided that the chicken-only name concept would inhibit growth, so they expanded the menu to include turkey, ham, and meat loaf, and changed the name to Boston Market. Lighter lunch fare was introduced under the name Boston Carver Sandwiches. The outlets also sold baked hams and rotisserie-roasted turkeys.

Future plans call for more than 3,500 restaurants to open in the next five to seven years, a total that will increase significantly when the chain goes international. Around the world everyone will be able to enjoy a home-cooked meal from Boston Market.

CURRENT SUCCESS
JACUZZI

ALL IN THE FAMILY

In the early 1900s, the seven Jacuzzi brothers, Candido, Gelindo, Giussepe, Franco, Valeriano, Giacondo, and Rachele, immigrated to San Francisco, California, from Italy. In America, they invented an enclosed cabin monoplane which brought them success in the aviation industry and made hydraulic water pumps for agricultural usage. In 1956, owing to a family member's need for daily hydrotherapy treatments, the company's engineers built an immersible in-home bathtub pump called the J-300. In 1968, Roy, one of the brothers' grandsons, adapted the J-300 pump as an in-tub whirlpool apparatus. It would add a new meaning to the phrase "taking a bath": **Jacuzzi.**

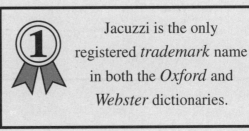

Jacuzzi is the only registered *trademark* name in both the *Oxford* and *Webster* dictionaries.

NATIONAL BATH TIMES

Ritual bathing dates back to ancient Egypt. The early Minoan civilization in the Aegean region introduced baths for the populace, and the Greeks luxuriated in baths by heating water and installing showers. The Romans were known for their glorious public bathhouses constructed of rich

mosaics, inlaid marble and gilded metals. Remnants of some of these great bath-houses stand at Caracalla outside Rome.

Public bathing was not part of any European culture after the decline of the Roman Empire. Communal bathing was seen as a health risk. It was no coincidence that a decline in bathing corresponded to the rise of perfumes, body scents, and nosegays.

But as more Europeans crowded into cities, large public bathing emporiums again became the norm. European immigrants to the United States in the 1880s brought the public bathing concept with them.

The baths on the Lower East Side of New York City were an example of public bathing on a grand scale. These existed as meeting places long after apartments routinely were built with private bathing facilities.

The most famous **Roman** bathing facility is in Bath, England, whose waters were called *aqua solis* (the waters of the sun) because they were heated by natural springs.

WATER WORKS

mericans in the 1960s became obsessed with health and fitness. Roy Jacuzzi, a recent University of California-Berkeley engineering graduate, had been appointed the Jacuzzi Company's head of Research and Development. He wisely surmised he could combine the company's long history and expertise in hydraulic water pumps with the burgeoning health and

fitness craze. After all, he thought, what better way to relax after a hard day's work or hard workout than a long soak in a hot tub?

Roy ordered the company's engineers to build a prototype whirlpool bath in 1968, a single-person unit named the Roman Bath. This was the first system made without a portable pump inside the tub. He took the model on the road to trade shows and fairs throughout the West. The sales pitch pointed out that, for the first time, bathers could enjoy a relaxing hydromassage in their own tub.

Early sales success encouraged Roy to take the Roman Bath to an industry trade show where it proved to be a big hit. He returned with a stack of orders, ending any family doubts about manufacturing the built-in whirlpool bath system.

TRIPPING THE TUB FANTASTIC

The Roman Bath unit was followed by the Adonis model, a two-person bathtub built in 1970. Greater publicity resulted from the development of its safe jet-air technology expanded to fit larger outdoor units called "hot tubs." Many of these tubs were made of California redwood and cedar, woods that would not deteriorate outdoors. The media reported the latest California fad: group bathing in a "Jacuzzi."

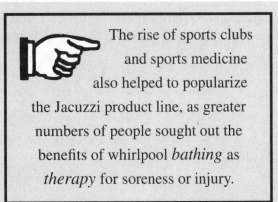

The rise of sports clubs and sports medicine also helped to popularize the Jacuzzi product line, as greater numbers of people sought out the benefits of whirlpool *bathing* as *therapy* for soreness or injury.

Nude bathing in hot tubs became a social event. A dinner in affluent Tiburon, northeast of San Francisco, often meant bringing a bottle of chardonnay and heading to the back yard for a late-night skinny dip in the large communal hot tub. Television and movies featured scenes of hot tub fun.

CURRENT SUCCESS

BATHS AND BEYOND

s the Jacuzzi company name became synonymous with whirlpool baths, it expanded to in-house and hot tub models offering a variety of colors, sizes, and shapes with different strength jet systems. The company also introduced extra products for massaging specific parts of the body; neck jets and seating contours.

The most recent Jacuzzi innovations include a series of shower systems that feature 16 hydrotherapy jets and multifunction, rotatable shower heads. Those fortunate enough to experience a power shower for the first time often giggle at the sheer pleasure of the pulse as water jets hit so many different body parts. These blasts of pressurized water are welcome therapy for bruises, sprains, tired muscles, and stress.

Jacuzzi dominates the industry. Roy owns more than 250 patents for innovations in whirlpool design and technology. The company has taken legal measures to protect the trademark so that it does not fall into generic use for all whirlpool baths and systems. In the future, consumers around the world will see more water-oriented products bearing the name Jacuzzi.

THE CHAIRMEN
LA-Z-BOY

COUNTRY COUSINS

Cousins Edwin Shoemaker and Edward Knabusch grew up in Monroe, Michigan, on Lake Erie. Shoemaker worked as a carpenter for a small manufacturing company, and Knabusch farmed. Both loved woodworking, and talked of someday starting a carpentry business. In 1927, they converted a garage into headquarters for a start-up furniture business: Kna-Shoe Manufacturing. The cousins' first creations were doll houses and wood cabinets, but sales were intermittent, and at times they made only $5 a week. The team also designed and constructed novelty furniture. One piece in particular, a wooden-slatted reclining porch chair, caught the eye of a furniture buyer in Toledo. He asked for one alteration: that the recliner be upholstered in fabric for indoor, year-round use. The **La-Z-Boy** was born.

> Some of the **rejected names** for the La-Z-Boy recliner were *Sit-N-Snooze, Slack-Back,* and *Comfort Carrier.*

THE CHAIRMEN

RELAXED SEATING

T he "easy chair" had its origins in the eighteenth century, the same era of the rocking chair (1766), which mimicked the design of the rocking horse created 50 years earlier.

Currently, more than 50 percent of recliner sales are to women. Recliners accounted for 6 million units in 1996.

The American recliner dates back to the Adirondack-style chairs and loungers used by tubercular patients in the late nineteenth century. These chairs first appeared in sanitariums where patients recuperated on "sun" porches, taking in the fresh air and at times even sleeping outside.

The Adirondack chair was famous for its wide slat backing, durability, and comfort. It was usually constructed from inexpensive pine, which meant it could be sold at an affordable price.

RECLINERS-R-US

S hoemaker and Knabusch patented their tilting chair design and hired the Toledo buyer's son Everett to be the company's first salesperson. The upholstered recliner debuted in 1929.

Floral City Furniture—as the cousins' business was now called—developed a reputation as the premiere reclining chair manufacturer. Their furniture's comfort was widely hailed. Because of the hard economic times, the cousins wisely

THE CHAIRMEN

bartered recliners to locals in exchange for livestock. By the end of the decade, Shoemaker had more animals than during his farming days, and Floral City Furniture survived the Depression.

Having seen the profit margins of retail stores, the cousins decided to open up their first store in downtown Monroe. To find a catchy name for the popular recliner, they sponsored a contest. The winning name— which said it all—was La-Z-Boy.

La-Z-Boy is listed in the *Guinness Book of World Records* because spokesperson Jim Backus did a world record 15,000 radio and TV commercials for them.

In the 1930s, the cousins' continued success depended upon the annual Furniture Show, which lured buyers from neighboring communities. The event—complete with circus tent, door prizes, Ferris wheels, and special attractions for children—swept Floral City Furniture into the big leagues.

In 1939, to maintain a competitive advantage, Shoemaker designed and patented a lever mechanism to adjust the chair's position. It was attached in a convenient spot on the side of the chair.

SEATING PLAN

During World War II the company had to forgo its business to build tank seats and crash pads. But in 1947, La-Z-Boy returned to full-time furniture production. The 1950s brought an unprecedented rise in the building of suburban homes, and an explosion in sales: Every man of the house wanted a comfortable La-Z-Boy recliner.

THE CHAIRMEN

In the 1960s, the company hired a series of suave celebrity spokesmen: Bing Crosby, Ed McMahon, and Johnny Carson all sat in the famous chair. The television commercials proved popular as well as profitable. But it was Jim Backus and his alter ego Mr. Magoo who captivated radio and television audiences, sending sales skyrocketing from $1 million in 1961 to $53 million a decade later. The introduction of the Reclina-Rocker in the late 1960s further increased La-Z-Boy's popularity.

> The oddest creation in La-Z-Boy history was an *all-mink loveseat* recliner designed to resemble a car seat.

SITTING PRETTY

Today, La-Z-Boy enjoys a dominant 75 percent share of the recliner market. Branching out into other areas, the company has become the third largest manufacturer of upholstered furniture in the country. The La-Z-Boy Furniture Galleries display coordinated "rooms" decorated with La-Z-Boy furniture. These galleries have higher sales per square foot than any other conventional furniture store.

Many regional furniture chains and large, single-store retailers feature La-Z-Boy Galleries due to the brand's appeal. Reportedly, 97 percent of American consumers surveyed recognized the La-Z-Boy name.

In an attempt to attract today's youthful shoppers, the company has implemented a "Make-A-Home" 800 number. Callers receive a free home decorating guide, in addition to the location of their nearest store. As long as people want to bask in the luxury of a reclining chair, Knabusch and Shoemaker's distinctly American creation will provide hours of slumber and comfort.

MORNING STAR

KELLOGG'S CORN FLAKES

FIRST FLAKES

In the 1820s and 1830s, New England Reverend Sylvester Graham was one of the first Americans to laud the virtues of a strictly vegetarian diet as a cure for intemperance. He praised the use of coarsely ground whole wheat flour; Graham flour was named for him. Eventually, his name would also be given to a tasty biscuit still popular today: the Graham Cracker. Rev. Graham preached the value of a healthy lifestyle and advocated frequent bathing, exercise, and abstinence from alcohol. His adherents were called Grahamites.

Dr. James Caleb Jackson was an ardent Grahamite whose preferred breakfast was cold cereal with milk. His meal attracted the attention of Dr. John Harvey Kellogg, who ran the Adventist Battle Creek Sanitarium in Michigan, a health "spa" for the nation's well-to-do.

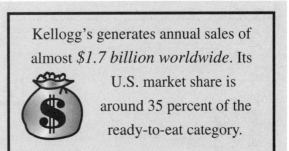

Kellogg's generates annual sales of almost *$1.7 billion worldwide*. Its U.S. market share is around 35 percent of the ready-to-eat category.

At the time, so-called health foods were not commercially available. Kellogg, who encouraged his clients to continue their healthy diets at home, produced such foods under the name of the Sanitas Food Company. He and his brother Will Keith—W.K.—had already developed granose, a wheat flake, in 1894, while

MORNING STAR

attempting to make an easier-to-digest bread. This flake would turn brother against brother and become the world's leading ready-to-eat breakfast cereal. Although both men would achieve fame and fortune, it is only W.K. whose name and signature are forever linked with **Kellogg's Corn Flakes**.

SIBLING RIVALRY

What began as sibling rivalry between the Kellogg boys would ignite a national ritual—starting each day with a bowl of grain cereal and milk. The Sanitas Company tried unsuccessfully to convert grains into cereals but all efforts crumbled. They then moved on to bread. The brothers attempted to run boiled wheat dough through roller presses, but the result was a gummy mess. One day, when the roller ground to a halt, the dough dried and broke off into thin wheat flakes. By 1895, Sanitas was turning out 100,000 pounds of flakes annually and selling a 10-ounce box for $.15.

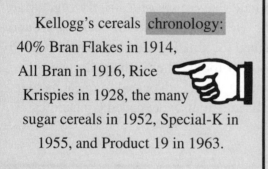

Kellogg's cereals chronology: 40% Bran Flakes in 1914, All Bran in 1916, Rice Krispies in 1928, the many sugar cereals in 1952, Special-K in 1955, and Product 19 in 1963.

POST PARTUM

Charles Wilson Post, a patient taking the "cure" at Battle Creek Sanitarium, often wandered the grounds on his daily constitutional. One day he stopped to watch the cereal flakes being made. The process intrigued him; he could see that the technology was relatively simple. When he returned home, he started the Postum Cereal Company, making a a hot drink called Postum and a nutty cereal called Grape-Nuts. By 1900, C.W. Post's cereal company generated $3 million in sales.

MORNING STAR

The Kellogg brothers were outraged when they learned of Post's cereal venture. Dr. John conceived the Sanitas Food Company as an altruistic venture, whose products were developed to help people's health. Within a year, more than two dozen companies had sprouted up in Battle Creek, making breakfast cereals from oats, wheat, rice, and other grain ingredients.

The brothers argued about the commercial objectives of the cereal. Dr. John wanted it to remain as an adjunct of the Sanitarium; W.K. wanted to sell as much granose to America as possible. In 1900, Sanitas moved to a new $50,000 facility, but Dr. John refused to pay his share, insisting he had never authorized the construction. This marked the beginning of the end of the brothers' working relationship.

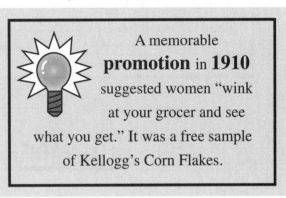

A memorable **promotion** in **1910** suggested women "wink at your grocer and see what you get." It was a free sample of Kellogg's Corn Flakes.

CEREAL NUMBERS

By 1906, W.K. Kellogg opened his own cereal company, the Battle Creek Toasted Corn Flake Company, and officially began to market the product as Corn Flakes. The company's name highlighted a new production method that resulted in a tastier and crunchier flake. By 1907, 2,900 cases of cereal were produced each day. Ever the entrepreneur, he spent heavily on advertising—spooning over $1 million into promotions by 1911.

After Dr. John renamed his company the Kellogg Sanitas Food Company, in 1909, W.K. sued his brother for the exclusive rights to use the family name. In the suit, W.K. accused John of copying his packaging styles and slogans.

MORNING STAR

Gradually, W.K. bought out his brother's stock in Sanitas and, by 1921, the name Kellogg was his alone. After 1922, when his company lost the rights to claim "Toasted Corn Flakes" as a trademark product name, W.K. reincorporated as the Kellogg Company.

An average of two new breakfast cereals are introduced every week in **America. Families** with teenage children spend more than $122 per year in cereal.

LIKE FATHER, LIKE SON

Sadly, the family feud did not end with the brothers. W.K.'s son John discovered a malting process that made the cereal flakes taste nutty. This resulted in All-Bran, a new cereal that promoted the Kellogg's name as the highest-quality cereal manufacturer. (John eventually would be credited with more than 200 patents and trademarks.)

Father and son survived the post-World War I food shortages when raw materials were hard to come by. But in 1920, the company suffered its only loss and rejected a competitor's buyout. Both W.K. and his son John worked six months without pay. But the hard times caused father and son to squabble incessantly, and in 1925 W.K. forced John out of the company.

Even after W.K. hired a new president to run the company in 1941, he remained its titular head. By 1948, company sales had reached $100 million, due to W.K.'s advertising and expansion strategy. W.K. Kellogg died in 1951 at the age of 91. In

MORNING STAR

addition to his business achievements, he had created the Kellogg's Foundation, which poured millions into agricultural, health, and educational institutions. The company had become the world's largest producer of ready-to-eat cereals as a result of a failed bread-making process.

SLICE OF LIFE
SWISS ARMY KNIFE

BLADE RUNNER

arl Elsener, born in 1860 in Zug, Switzerland, was a master craftsman who organized the Association of Swiss Master Cutlers in 1890. The first order of business for the guild was to make a knife for Swiss soldiers. Until then, the Swiss used knives made in Germany.

The Swiss Army knife was made in red so that, if dropped in the snow, it could be easily spotted.

Elsener's first creation was delivered in 1891. The "soldier's knife" contained a long blade, screwdriver, reamer, and can opener. He continued making variations of this basic prototype: the schoolboy's, farmer's, and, finally, his masterpiece, the officer's knife.

Elsener patented the Swiss Officer's Knife in 1897. It was a lighter and more elegant version of the soldier's model, featuring four attachments plus a corkscrew and a smaller blade. By 1909, the little knife's popularity was evidenced by the rash of European imitators. To thwart competitors, Elsener established brand identity. He named his company Victorinox to honor his mother Victoria. To honor his country, he stamped the national emblem, the Swiss Cross, on the handle: **Swiss Army Knife**.

SLICE OF LIFE

THE AMERICAN PLAN

T he Victorinox Officer's Knife, *Offizersmessier* in German, was popular in Europe, but it was not until American forces arrived during World War II that the knife attracted worldwide attention. U.S. troops found the knife in the PX shops, where it proved a great buy. Since the English-speaking Yanks could not pronounce *Offizersmessier,* they just asked for the "Swiss Army Knife."

After the war, orders from America trickled to Switzerland, mainly from high-quality cutlery stores. In 1960, the knife received some notoriety when the Russians displayed the Swiss Army Knife taken from downed U-2 pilot Gary Powers and called it standard CIA spy issue. But in 1974, sales in the U.S. totaled only $800,000.

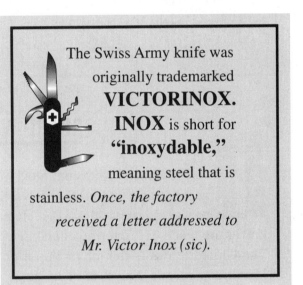

The Swiss Army knife was originally trademarked **VICTORINOX. INOX** is short for **"inoxydable,"** meaning steel that is stainless. *Once, the factory received a letter addressed to Mr. Victor Inox (sic).*

Over the years, the company added more blades and sold different models. Some additions to the basic six attachments were a wood saw, scissors, tweezers, toothpicks, nail file, Phillips screwdriver, fish scaler, and hook disgorger. The world's best-seller is the Swiss Champion, loaded with 16 blades and 24 tools, including a wire cutter and ruler.

The rise of the knife's popularity in America is attributed to the promotion and sales efforts of the Forschner Group, cutlery marketing specialists who have imported Victorinox butcher knives since the 1930s. In 1975, Forschner introduced the knife to quality cutlery stores like Hoffritz and to high-priced hunting, camping, and outdoor catalogs. By 1981, American sales reached $11 million.

SLICE OF LIFE

The appeal of the versatile little red knife is twofold: its portability and utilitarian functions have many daily uses, and its compact size and intriguing delivery system delight its owners. Former U.S. presidents Lyndon Johnson and George Bush (who printed the presidential seal on the knives and gave them as gifts) were fans. Astronauts discovered it was the ideal, multifunctional tool. The knife is so popular in the U.S. that there is even a 2,300-member Swiss Army Knife Society based in San Diego, whose motto is *Semper Versatilis*.

> It's the thought that counts: Eli Lilly & Company ordered a Swiss Army knife made with a special curved blade that could be used to perform tracheotomies. It was given as a promo gift to doctors.

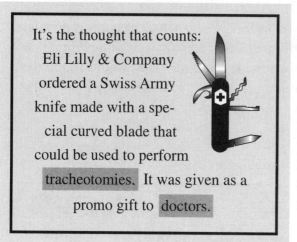

SHARP WITTED

he Forschner Group continued to expand sales in the 1980s and 1990s without any appreciable advertising. Word-of-mouth praise for the product caused sales to escalate. Today, some 6 million Swiss Army knives are made by Victorinox annually; 80 percent are designated for export. The United States is the major importer at $10 million yearly. Interestingly, Victorinox spends 2 percent of its gross sales pursuing and prosecuting less-expensive imitators.

The knife has played a part in many exciting rescue stories, novels, and parodies:

- A North Carolina anesthesiologist used the six-blade knife to perform surgery on an airplane passenger choking on food.
- The murderer in Lawrence Sander's mystery thriller *The Third Deadly Sin* is a woman who cuts her lovers' throats with a Victorinox.

- A Johnny Carson skit featured a 6-foot knife with an interesting attachment: a full-size rubber woman.
- A *Saturday Night Live* sketch introduced the New York City Swiss Army Knife, complete with submachine gun.
- In a *New Yorker* cartoon, a full-size couch opened out as a blade.

At the Museum of Modern Art in Manhattan, Victorinox's Swiss Army Knife is exhibited in the museum's exclusive selection of "Good Industrial Designs."

SWISS HEIR

What does the future hold for the knife now owned by more than 150 million people? Ideas for new attachments and tools pour into Victorinox every year. These range from the absurd—a power saw and a food mixer—to the practical—a small flashlight. Can a computer chip or some miniature communication device be far behind?

Karl Elsener's family continues to lead the company to this day. He would be proud of the reputation for quality that is associated with his creation. He also would be delighted to learn that the German Army buys a special green model from Victorinox for its troops. Today, the Germans use a Swiss Army Knife.

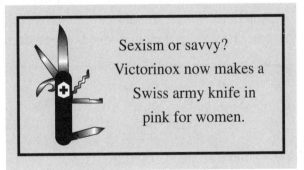

Sexism or savvy? Victorinox now makes a Swiss army knife in pink for women.

HILL OF BEANS
STARBUCKS

NECTAR FROM THE GODS

merican coffee aficionados long dreamed of coffeehouses with gleaming white-marble polished counters, where white-coated servers made steaming cups of robust coffee one cup at a time. These magical coffee rooms would produce delicious concoctions with mellifluous names that trilled off the tongue: Caffè Latte, Espresso Macchiato, Caffè Mocha, and Espresso Con Panna. In these coffee lovers' dream palaces, even a mundane cup of drip coffee would unlock the hidden magic of the coffee bean.

It seemed unlikely that such a coffee-rich fantasy could realize itself on American shores. But after a visit to Milan, Italy, with its 1,700 gleaming espresso bars, Howard Schultz believed he could make it happen, and in 1985 opened his first coffee bar in Seattle called Il Giornale. Schultz used coffee from his former employers, a northwest retail roasting operation called **Starbucks**.

> Starbucks' goal for the year 2000 is to be a *billion-dollar* company with stores worldwide.

HILL OF BEANS

FOR PEET'S SAKE

lfred Peet, a Dutchman living in the U.S., remembered the deliciously roasted high-grade arabica beans that he bought in Holland. In 1966, he opened Peet's Coffee in Berkeley, California, introducing never-heard-before coffees to an eager American clientele. Over time, coffee addicts on the Pacific Coast considered this shop mecca.

Zev Siegl, a partner in a would-be coffee shop venture, made a pilgrimage from Seattle in 1972 to see Peet and to listen to his coffeemaking wisdom. Siegl was one of three investors who had raised a total of $11,000 to open a coffee shop in Seattle. The other two were Gordon Bowker, a magazine writer, and Jerry Baldwin, a schoolteacher like Siegl.

The partners decided to name the shop Starbucks after the coffee-loving first mate in Herman Melville's classic *Moby Dick*. In keeping with the nautical theme, a two-tailed siren was made part of the company logo. For the first nine months, they purchased their coffee beans from Peet's and enticed customers with free cups.

Then they began to roast their own beans; Baldwin became the company's first roaster. By 1982, Starbucks had opened five stores in Washington, and operated a roasting facility that sold to restaurants. As perfectionists who continued to follow Peet's rules, they knew that the shelf life of coffee was only 14 days after roasting, so the company donated outdated coffee to charity.

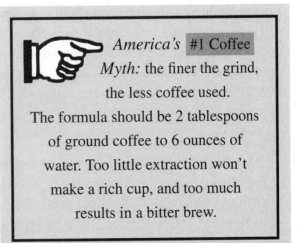

America's #1 Coffee
Myth: the finer the grind, the less coffee used.
The formula should be 2 tablespoons of ground coffee to 6 ounces of water. Too little extraction won't make a rich cup, and too much results in a bitter brew.

HILL OF BEANS

THE PERFECT BLEND

 n 1982, 10 years after opening the first store, the company hired a New Yorker named Howard Schultz to oversee its expanding operation. Schultz had been a vice president of Hammarplast, a Swedish housewares company. After a trip to Seattle, he was impressed with the company and the "clean" life of the Northwest.

Three years later, in 1985, Schultz was sent to Italy on a bean-buying trip. While strolling through Milan, he became intrigued by the espresso bars that dotted every street. He was impressed with the delicious taste of coffee made from gleaming copper and aluminum espresso machines. And he noticed that the bars were social gathering places for the Milanese.

> **What is espresso?**
> Coffee brewed by forcing steam through finely ground darkly roasted coffee beans.

Schultz, returned to America as an espresso bar zealot. He presented his idea of reproducing the bars to the Starbucks' owners, but they did not share his vision. He persisted and, in 1984, the coffee bar concept was tested in a Seattle Starbucks location, where it proved an immediate hit. A year later Schultz opened his first espresso bar, called Il Giornale. Seed money came from investors and the Starbucks owners, who were happy to see their brand used exclusively in the store.

Starbucks bought out Peet's five-store California operation in 1985, but the timing proved disastrous because the wholesale coffee market had become inundated with flavored coffees. Starbucks resolutely refused to include what they regarded as flavored coffee aberrations in its retail stores. By 1987, after 15 years selling

gourmet coffee, the business had lost its luster, and the owners became interested in other ventures; Siegl had already left in 1980, and Bowker wanted to launch Red Hook Ale.

Who should come knocking at the door with an intriguing buyout proposition? None other than former employee Howard Schultz, by then the owner of 11 successful Il Giornale espresso bars in Washington, Vancouver, and Chicago. His offer: $4 million for the company. The deal was struck, with Baldwin staying on as president of the retail subsidiary. Overnight, all the Il Giornale stores changed their names to the more recognizable Starbucks.

THE SAUCER'S APPRENTICE

One key to Schultz's overall goal—to introduce Starbucks throughout the United States—was to find and train personnel who would jump on the Starbucks' quality bandwagon. His motto: "Hire people smarter than you and get out of their way." But before the company could get out of the way, new employees had to be instructed in the intricacies of making many permutations of coffee one cup at a time. The training process to become a *barista* requires 24 hours of classroom instruction and 30 hours-plus of hands-on, on-site experience.

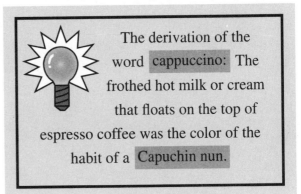

The derivation of the word cappuccino: The frothed hot milk or cream that floats on the top of espresso coffee was the color of the habit of a Capuchin nun.

The efficient Starbucks system separates the ordering procedure into a three-step process: coffee drink-calling, coffee drink-making, and cup management. The barista must be able to master an eight-attribute list: type, quantity, size, flavoring, number of espresso shots, kind of milk, foam

consistency, and the name of the drink. There are always three baristas involved in any customer's individual request: one at the machine who makes the coffee, a second who foams milk, and the third at the cash register.

THEIR CUP RUNNETH OVER

Numbers reveal Starbucks to be a retail phenomenon. In 1987, the company numbered 11 stores; less than 10 years later, it had multiplied to 850. In that time frame, Schultz hired experienced information and management experts from the fast-food industry to supervise the expansion.

In 1996, Starbucks opened its first overseas store in Tokyo, hoping that the trendy Japanese would also want to quaff frappuccinos and caffè mochas. The most risky plan is to open the chain in Europe—especially in Italy, where there are already more than 200,000 espresso bars.

THE BIG CHILL
BEN & JERRY'S ICE CREAM

THE PERFECT FRIENDSHIP

Ben Cohen and Jerry Greenfield became friends in the 7th grade, where they were the widest boys in gym class. In college, Jerry got an A in a course called Carnival Techniques, excelling at fire-eating and cinder-block smashing. Ben was a college drop-out who held some unusual part-time jobs including egg separator, supermarket floor mopper, and night watchman at a race track. From such inauspicious beginnings, they teamed up to find a fun business that would enable them to be their own bosses and to work when, where, and how they wanted.

One of them suggested a food venture, since bagels and ice cream were their passions. The bagel idea became UBS (United Bagel Service), which they imagined would be a delivery service to homes and offices. But after one phone call to price a bagel-making machine, they decided to go into the ice cream business. They applied for a $5 mail-order course in ice cream making from Penn State, and received a perfect score on the final (it was an open book test). With "degrees" in hand, they looked around for a college town with a warm climate and no ice cream parlor. Well, they got the "no ice cream parlor" right anyhow: They ended up in Burlington, Vermont, which "boasts" an average of 161 days a year that the temperature drops below freezing, and opened **Ben & Jerry's.**

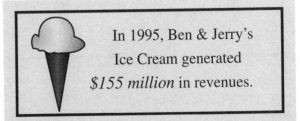

In 1995, Ben & Jerry's Ice Cream generated *$155 million* in revenues.

THE BIG CHILL

THEY ALL SCREAM FOR ICE CREAM

Ice cream, the sweet frozen confection made from milk fat, sugar, flavoring, and on occasion, eggs, nuts, and fruits, had its beginnings as flavored ice as far back as ancient Rome. Italian ices and gelati are still hugely popular today.

In the United States, the manufacture of ice cream on a commercial scale began in Baltimore in 1851. With the implementation of the pasteurization and homogenization processes, it was made safe for mass consumption. But not until it was packaged in individual servings of Dixie Cups in the 1920s that ice cream achieved popularity on a grand scale.

After World War II, improved and larger freezer compartments in modern refrigerators made it possible to store ice cream purchased from supermarket freezer sections, and demand increased. Regional brands dominated their local markets: Breyers in New York City, Knudsons in Los Angeles, and the Dove Bar in Chicago.

In the 1960s, an enterprising easterner would take the vanilla, chocolate, and strawberry classics, add more fat and a greater variety of flavors, and convert mundane bulk ice cream into Häagen-Dazs, a gourmet delight at a gourmet price.

Ben & Jerry's Ice Cream made the world's biggest sundae consisting of 10 tons of ice cream.

THE BIG CHILL

BIRTH OF A NOTION

The boys moved to Burlington in the fall of 1977, where they rented an abandoned gasoline station. They named the company Ben & Jerry's simply because it sounded better than Jerry & Ben's. As consolation, Jerry was made president. In the early months, while they renovated the station, they learned firsthand about the food business by selling hot cider, coffee, and oatmeal cookies to a local pottery store. They met customers, and entertained them with jigsaw puzzles and games, and instituted one of the trademarks of their later business: They gave away the cookies free.

Ben and Jerry experimented with making ice cream, sometimes achieving rich and creamy results; other times creating concoctions that bounced or stretched. Neither success nor failure deterred the partners from consuming everything they made. In 1978, they pooled their resources, and with $12,000 in cash ($4,000 of it borrowed), they opened Ben & Jerry's Homemade Ice Cream Scoop Shop.

Two of Ben & Jerry's flavors are named **for rock stars:** Cherry Garcia and Wavy Gravy.

At the shop, a friend played honky-tonk piano while customers ordered. He also wrote a song for the ice cream entrepreneurs called the *Ice Cream Blues* ("I like homemade ice cream but I don't like standing in line. Down at Ben & Jerry's, well, I'll wait any old time. Diddy wah, Diddy wah, doooo . . .").

THE BIG CHILL

CHUNK FOOD

Ben felt there was something missing in the ice cream—chunks! Chunks of fruit, chunks of nuts, chunks of candy bars, chunks and chunks of chunks. Jerry liked smooth ice cream accented with little flecks of flavoring. He argued that ice cream made with large chunks could produce a spoonful that was all ice cream and no chunk. Ben, an optimist, countered that if one spoonful came up empty, the next one would have a huge chunk.

Chunk or no chunk, the shop was doing nonstop business, scooping 1,000 cones on a hot day. On occasion, they ran out of ice cream before closing time and placed the international "no ice cream" sign (an ice cream cone with a red slash through it) on the door. On Mother's Day, they gave out free cones to all mothers, and two cones to pregnant women. Their first attempt at attracting a crowd was to make a gigantic Cherries Jubilee for 2,000 people. Their headline-making stunts culminated in the creation of the world's largest sundae, a 20,000-pound monstrosity made in and by the town of St. Albans, Vermont.

New Ben & Jerry ice cream shop owners attend *Scoop U.*

THE BIG SCOOP

The business expanded when a Burlington restaurant asked if the shop would be its ice cream supplier. Naturally, the Ben and Jerry obliged. They figured others might be interested, so Ben packed up samples in his old VW and visited restaurants and grocery stores, offering 12 flavors. Finally, they purchased a 1969 ice cream truck and painted the sides with a colorful child-like drawing. The design featured two huge arms running down the sides and meeting in the back holding two gigantic ice cream cones.

THE BIG CHILL

The shop became too small to meet the increased demand, and the company moved into a larger location, where 12 people worked daily making and packing pints of ice cream. Clearly, it was time to open shop in Boston. They were an immediate hit there, too.

But not everyone in Boston welcomed them with open arms. The Pillsbury Company, owners of Häagen-Dazs, warned distributors that if they wanted to continue selling the super-lucrative Häagen Dazs line, they could not sell Ben & Jerry's. The ensuing legal battle was settled out of court, but not before the small-timers from Vermont brought the mammoth from Minnesota to its public relations knees by printing bumper stickers asking, "What's the Doughboy Afraid Of?" And Jerry appointed himself a one-person picket line at Pillsbury headquarters, where he chatted with employees and distributed literature.

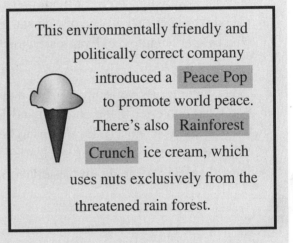

This environmentally friendly and politically correct company introduced a Peace Pop to promote world peace. There's also Rainforest Crunch ice cream, which uses nuts exclusively from the threatened rain forest.

With the Pillsbury obstacle removed, nothing stood in the way of further regional and national expansion. In 1984, Ben and Jerry were named "National Ice Cream Retailer(s) of the Year." To promote their products and, as always, to have fun, they embarked on a four-month trip in the "Cowmobile," an altered mobile home, and distributed free ice cream cones. But the vehicle accidentally burned to the ground, after which Ben quipped they had made the largest baked Alaska in history.

THE BIG CHILL

STATE OF THE UNION

Ben and Jerry also share a social conscience; they donate a percentage of their profits to charities. In 1985, they established the Ben & Jerry Foundation, which awards more than $350,000 to worthwhile groups. The foundation receives 7.5 percent of the company's annual pretax profit.

Another policy that brought them national attention was the company salary scale, which states that no one person can make more than five times the wages of the lowest-paid employee. Eventually, this would rise to a multiple of seven.

Today, having survived something of a meltdown in sales due to the ice cream's high fat and cholesterol content, Ben and Jerry are still having fun. They opened two scoop shops in Russia. It remains to be seen how flavors like Cherry Garcia, Chunky Monkey, or Aztec Harvest Coffee translate into Russian. But however it sounds, there will be no doubt these flavors come from Ben & Jerry's.

POCKET BOOK
FILOFAX

GRACE UNDER FIRE

During World War II, the London-based Norman and Hill Company never considered itself a prime target for the Luftwaffe. It produced only a small, compact notebook hardly threatening to the Nazis. But stray German bombs razed the building during a December 1940 blitz, and the company and its records were in shambles. The outlook appeared bleak; it would take months before executives could reconstruct the client and supplier lists. While her coworkers stared despondently at the bombed-out site, Grace Scurr appeared waving a notebook in her hand. It contained all the commercial information the company needed to re-start business that day! Grace, who had arrived as a temp in 1928 with the intention of staying only a few weeks, had remained with the company as a secretary. It was she who coined the name for the pocket organizer when it was registered as a trademark in 1930. Thus it was only fitting that the person who had christened the product would save the company by using the organizer precisely in the way it was intended, to file and keep information: **Filofax.**

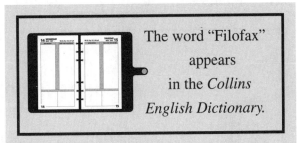

The word "Filofax" appears in the *Collins English Dictionary*.

POCKET BOOK

YOUR HEART BELONGS TO DATA

ry to imagine your great-grandparents' era. They may not even have had a telephone number. To reach someone on the new-fangled contraption, they cranked it up and asked the lone switchboard operator to "Ring up the Lloyds on Gibbs Lane."

Today to contact the Lloyds, you need their home, country home, car, or cellular phone, *and* fax numbers—plus their e-mail address. To send mail, you need their zip code or zip plus-four number sequence.

How is anyone supposed to keep track of all those numbers? *And* keep tabs on concert or show tickets? Dry cleaning receipts? Laundry tickets? Credit cards? Health club identification? Driver's license? How about a calendar to write in appointments, meetings, birthdays, and anniversaries? Having one central location for all this information has become a modern-day necessity.

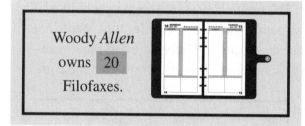

Woody *Allen* owns 20 Filofaxes.

ORGANIZED CHAOS

he Norman and Hill Company of London opened for business in 1921, when printer William Rounce and stationer Posseen Hill joined forces to market a small organizational system that featured segmented compartments for date- and record-keeping. In its formative years, until 1933, most of the purchasers consisted of a loyal group of journalists, clergymen, lawyers, and medical practitioners. This handy calf's leather organizer was just what busy people needed. Each new year, the owners would replace the outdated appointment calendar with a new one; the old was maintained as a permanent record.

During World War II, the notebook was widely used by the military; officers found it invaluable for tracking plans and data. It became a compulsory purchase of officers passing through the British Army's Staff College in Camberley. It even was given a Latin nickname, *vade mecum,* meaning "always with you." A special insert was created for the soldiers, called "Troop Commanders Bible."

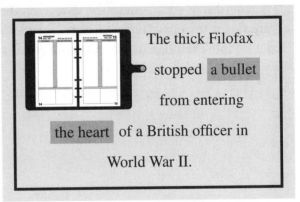

The thick Filofax stopped a bullet from entering the heart of a British officer in World War II.

KING DAVID

In 1959, David Collischon purchased a Filofax. He became an enthusiastic user of the product, and asked the key question: "Why has the Filofax not been marketed to a wider international audience?"

Subsequently, Collischon approached Norman and Hill in 1972, and became one of their U.S. wholesalers. He and his wife Lesley started a company called Pocketfax and, during the next eight years, used direct mail to sell Filofax, effectively introducing it to thousands of American customers.

BOOK VALUE

By 1980, the Collischons had enough capital to purchase Norman and Hill, which then was earning a scant $225,000 annually. Seven years later, the new company generated $27 million, and, by 1996, it rose dramatically to over $50 million.

The reason for the dramatic rise in sales? The American thirtysomething "work is what I live for" generation discovered in the Filofax the perfect one-source organizer for busy lives. Also, women adopted the organizer because it fit perfectly into their handbags and attaché cases.

ACKNOWLEDGMENTS

THE HOUSE THAT RUTH BUILT

We are indebted foremost to Ruth Mills, Senior Editor of the Professional, Reference, and Trade Group at John Wiley and Sons, Inc. She conceived of this book after having read the *New York Times*'s obituary (by Robert McG. Thomas) of Edward Lowe, the inventor of Kitty Litter. Mills offered brilliant suggestions and continuous encouragement. Her unflagging enthusiasm for the project lifted our spirits at every step. She is deservedly the mother of this book's invention.

THE MATCHMAKER

We were introduced to Mills by our wonderful friend Jo-Ann Wasserman, an editor at John Wiley & Sons.

THE MARVELOUS LIST GATHERERS

Some special people spent effort gathering us lengthy lists of possible products. Our heartfelt thanks to: Joie Smith, Carol Freeman Taffet, Eric R. Fox, Jane Gaillard, Ella Lippman Kelly, Peter Thompson, Carol Benjamin, Jed Spingarn, and Ann Cohen.

MARKETING AND ADVERTISING ASSOCIATES

Many of the product stories were measurably improved by contacting old acquaintances: Bruce Kelly, Ari Kopelman, Bruce Alpert, Joe O'Donnell, Janice Lee, Joe Froschl, and Robert Wagar.

ACKNOWLEDGMENTS

HELPFUL FRIENDS

Em and Bal Golden, Kathy Green, Harold, Dave and Jean Green, Julie and Doug Donaldson, Marian Davis, Carol Bugge, Tim Mullen, Danny Deutch, Victoria Lang, Louis Milgrom, Naomi Wax, David Kumin, Mike Blaxill, Debbie Andrews, Rusty Magee, Dr. Sidney Love, Francis Gasparini, Jack Feldman, Miho Cha, Chris Divine, The Adlers, Mike Davis, Joel Wassermann, Rick Hoffer, Ann Gordon, Scott and Therese Garsson, Elly Eisenberg, Amanda Green, Dr. James Hudson, Bob and Mary Hogan, Peter Golden, David Lai, Sean Kelly, The Rogges, Andy Woo, Michael Shalhoub, Paul and Betsy Rosengren, The Medweds, Emily Sachar, Seth and Barbara Zimmerman, Matti Leshem, Rich Campbell, Jack Mason, Gary Negbauer, John Werber, Nancy Sachar, Ed Kaczmarek, Hal Negbaeur, Guy Maxtone-Graham, Tony Hoylan, Christine and Finbarr Murphy, Judy and Bob Greber, Karen and Steve Berkenfeld, Betty Lev, Christine and Steven Rhodes, Pat Ellis, Marian and Edward Last, Maureen and Jim Duke, Ron Davis, Sandra Small, Caroline and Richard McDonough, Ann Patch, Patricia H. and Charles Clarkson, Carrie and William Rosenthal, Suzanne and Richard Lewis, Ed Hughes, Charles Hodgson, Mark Kaminsky, Vincent Izzo, Marvin Peck, Dr. Bruce Ettinger, David Toser, Cynthia Jenner, Sara and Geoffrey Thompson, Molly Rhodes, Fran Davis, Marcia Shrock, and Monika Jain (at Wiley)

ANIMAL ASSISTANTS

Zoli & Elwood

BIBLIOGRAPHY

Browser's Book of Beginnings
  Charles Panati
  Houghton Mifflin Company, Boston, 1984

Encyclopedia of Consumer Brands, Volumes I, II, and III
  St. James Press, Detroit, MI, 1994

The Evolution of Useful Things
  Henry Petroski
  Vintage Books, New York, 1994

Great Modern Inventions
  Gerald Méssadi
  W & R Chambers Ltd., Edinburgh, England, 1991

How the Cadillac Got Its Fins
  Jack Mingo
  Harperbusiness/A Division of Harpercollins, New York, 1994

International Directory of Company Histories, Volumes 1—16
  St. James Press, Detroit, MI, 1996

New Product Success Stories
  Robert J. Thomas
  John Wiley & Sons, Inc., New York, 1995

Notable Corporate Chronologies, Volumes I and II
  Susan Boyles Martin, Editor
  Gale Research Inc., an International Thomson Publishing Co., Detroit, MI, 1995

BIBLIOGRAPHY

Panati's Extraordinary Origins of Everyday Things
  Charles Panati
  Harper & Row, New York, 1987

Walker's Corporate Directory of U.S. Public Companies
  Walker's Research, LLC, E. Tollenaere Walsh, Publisher, San Mateo, CA, 1997

INDEX

Band-Aid   56

Barbie   113

Beltone   167

Ben & Jerry's Ice Cream   225

Bic   122

Boston Market   199

Clairol   126

The Club   70

Crayola   185

Cuisinart, Inc.   74

The Dirt Devil 109

Dixie Cups   180

Duncan Yo-Yo   5

Elmer's All-Purpose Glue   20

Ex-Lax   16

Filofax   231

Frito-Lay   156

Gerber   146

Hallmark, Inc.   60

Heinz Ketchup   31

Jacuzzi   203

Jello-O   117

Kellogg's Corn Flakes   211

Kitty Litter   41

La-Z-Boy   207

L'eggs   151

Lego   87

Levi Strauss & Company   95

Liquid Paper   36

Melitta, Inc.   1

Midas   83

NordicTrack   65

Pampers   162

Post-It Notes   176

Rollerblades, Inc.   104

Silly Putty   51

Singer Sewing Machine   194

Slinky   136

S.O.S   172

Starbucks   220

INDEX

Swiss Army Knife   216

Tabasco Sauce   131

Tampax   46

Thermos   141

Tootsie Roll   190

Trivial Pursuit   91

Trojan Condoms   25

Tupperware   10

Vaseline   78

Velcro   99